Ivy

... some say she's poison

By

Deidra D. S. Green

Ivy: Some Say she's Poison

Other Books by Deidra D. S. Green:

- Elite Affairs I: Orchestrated Beauty
- Elite Affairs II: Simple Elegance
- Suddenly Single: So Undeserving
- From the Outside In
- Twisted Sister
- Twisted Sister II: Twisted's Revenge
- Twisted Sister III: After the Twist
- Woman at the Top of the Stairs

- Woman at the Top of the Stairs II: Sweet Revenge
- Woman at the Top of the Stairs III: The Final Say
- A Letter to My Mother (Four Part Letter Series)
- Exiting Gracefully
- Sick, Sicker, Sickest
- Interstate 64

Visit Deidra D. S. Green at http://deidrawrites.weebly.com/

Read Deidra's Blog at http://deidrawrites.weebly.com/

Follow Deidra on Twitter- @deidrag

Join Deidra on FB at http://www.facebook.com/deidra.d.green

Acknowledgements

It is such a blessing to be able to share my innermost thoughts, wild crazy stories, and true to life tales with my reading family. Although there are times when the words don't seem to come, I know I have been given a tremendous opportunity that sometimes requires me be patient. I recognize I am merely the conduit by which these stories come through, so I am learning, even as I am writing these words, that patience is necessary. I also thank my reading family for being patient with me and supporting me when the product is finished. Your support means more than you know. I can't say thank you enough.

I thank the Creator for the love of words. I thank the Creator for choosing me to do this passionate work. I send a heartfelt thank you to my Rathsi Publishing family who has been with me since my first book was published. Thank you to my literary team for this particular book.

I know I say it all the time but a heartfelt and endless thank you is extended to the loves of my life, VcToryann C'mone and Kamerron DeAnthony Alexander. Without you understanding my need for alone time and being so unimaginably supportive, none of this would happen. I love you both beyond the moon and stars…

Dedication

… This book is dedicated to the women who recognize the Ivy within…

Chapter One

...poison...

"Harder, fuck me harder."

This was not a request. She was not begging, not leading for greater satisfaction. This was a demand...unequivocally.

Brock did as he was told. He would do anything to please her; he loved her just that much. Holding on to Ivy's tight waist, Brock plunged his stiff cock deeper inside her, his ball sac slapping rhythmically against her ass. Parker, lying on the bed in front of the twosome kissed Ivy's luscious lips. She loved Ivy too and would do anything and everything to please her. Parker smiled as she cupped Ivy's breasts, pinching and twirling the nipples between her fingers. Ivy lifted her hand and placed it on Parker's shoulder, pushing downward. Parker responded and slid further down as Ivy encouraged her; moving her hand to Parker's head and cupping it as Parker's mouth found Ivy's plump breast. Once satisfied, Ivy allowed her hand to trace Parker's silhouette and toward her inner thigh. Parker needed no encouragement in opening her legs, lifting one and placing it on Ivy's undulating hip. Ivy slid her fingers into Parker's jewel box and her touch made Parker gasp; momentarily releasing Ivy's breast. Seeing the two women sexually entangled fueled Brock even more. The fire from his loins grew as he neared ejaculation.

"I'm cummin'…" he said breathlessly.

Ivy titillated Parker's pearl. Ivy mimicked Brock's rhythm and Parker panted, also nearing the verge of explosion.

"Ivy, can I cum, please…please Ivy," Parker begged; her back arching.

Brock grunted loudly as he exploded inside Ivy; his hot gism coated her throbbing clit. Parker squealed in ecstasy as she too reached her climax, riding the wave of Ivy's magical touch. And just like wounded soldiers, the two collapsed to the bed on either side of the one they loved. Ivy allowed them to languish for just a minute; each holding on to her as if she were their anchor. She then exited the bed and made her way to the shower.

No further words were necessary. Each knew what was expected. They had both been there before; whether singularly or plurally. Parker and Brock gathered their belongings and left the 6,000-square foot, luxury apartment. There was no exiting salutation between the two of them, just a slight smile as they went their separate ways. They would see Ivy again, but only when she wanted to see them. Most likely either or both of them would receive a text. A time would be given, nothing more. They would come running without hesitation. It's who she was and what she wanted. They accepted without question. Ivy had that kind of effect on people.

"Mama, when is daddy coming home?" This was a question Ivy asked often. Although they were an intact family, Ivy's father was not always around.

"Ivy, your father will be here when he gets here," her mother, Geneva reminded her. It was the fifth or sixth time Geneva answered the same question and she would continue to answer her one and only child. She knew how close Ivy was to her father. That's what she always wanted; for the two of them to have a good relationship. Ivy sulked in partial anticipation and some disappointment from the fact that her desires were not immediately met. Her mother busied five-year-old Ivy with alphabets to trace and books to color in, but Ivy wasn't focused on anything but the front door where she hoped her dad would soon appear.

An hour passed. Three hours later than he should have arrived, the front door opened. Her father was home.

"Hey, hey… where's daddy's little princess?"

Before the words were out of his mouth, Ivy was out of her chair, running full speed toward him. The smile on her face said it all. No matter how long she waited or how sad she'd previously been, the sight of her father made all things right. Geneva smiled as she looked upon the two most important people in her life. Ivy hugged her dad's knees so tight he couldn't move. Michael looked up from his daughter and saw his wife gazing in their direction. Michael offered Geneva a wayward smile. There was no apology there. He never owed her that. He wasn't just late for Ivy; he was late for dinner with his family; the dinner Geneva laboriously slaved over to ensure it was hot when her husband came home. The dinner that stood lukewarm on the stove. She put a plate in the oven to keep his portion warm, but she turned that off hours ago when she realized it was going to be another one of those nights. Still, seeing the two of them together made her heart glad. That's really what it was all about, right?

Michael didn't bother to take a step further into the modest, two bedroom, apartment the three of them shared. Instead, he offered to make it up to Ivy with ice cream. She eagerly accepted the suggestion and let go of his legs long enough to put on her shoes.

"Bye, mama," Ivy called as she grabbed her father's hand and exited the apartment. And Michael would have made good on his promise of ice cream, but only after making a necessary detour. Young Ivy peered out of the backseat window trying to see where the car stopped. She didn't see the ice cream parlor.

"Daddy," Ivy began.

"Just a minute, baby girl," her father interjected before the question could be raised. "This will only take a minute.

Ivy had no choice but to be content with her father's response. Michael blew the horn and stepped out of the vehicle. Before long, the door to the apartment building opened and a woman stepped out. She smiled as she descended the stairs upon reaching Michael, who was leaning against his 1990 Cadillac Seville. She threw her arms around his neck, their bodies pressed close together. Young Ivy watched as the woman kissed her dad on the mouth for what seemed like forever. Ivy saw her father's arms wrapped tightly around the woman's waist. She saw how her dad smiled as the two chatted with their lips almost touching. The woman didn't seem to notice Ivy in the backseat of the car. Maybe she was so smitten with Ivy's dad that she didn't have time for such things.

When the door of the apartment opened again, Ivy's attention followed. Two boys, dressed in matching, striped shirts came bolting down the stairs. They headed straight for her dad and greeted him with big smiles and hugs too. Ivy's face pressed against the glass; her breath causing the window to slightly fog and then dissipate as she breathed in and out. Ivy's dad reached his hand down and embraced the boys as they chatted eagerly. Ivy couldn't really hear what they were saying. She couldn't fully make out the words and her young mind couldn't completely comprehend what she saw. But she did hear the boys say 'dad'… a word she recognized… a word she used to describe the man standing outside the car… the dad she thought belonged only to her.

It was one of the boys who noticed Ivy in the back of the car and inquired of his father as to who the little girl was. Ivy didn't pay attention to the fact that the woman standing outside the car smiled an all-knowing smile as Michael opened the back door and reached in the car to pick up his daughter.

"Michael Jr., Thomas, this is your sister Ivy," Michael Sr. stated. His statement was without equivocation or explanation. The woman smiled again and made nice with Ivy, complimenting on how cute she was while touching her long pony tails. The boys offered a confused hello and Ivy waved at them. They too thought they were the only ones. There would be questions for their mother later, but for the moment they accepted their father's word for what it was. The children looked at each other as the adults continued to talk. They saw things about the other that reminded them of who they were. They would weigh and measure the content of the other but wouldn't speak a word, at least not at the moment. The word dad was old to each of them, but new in reference to this other person, these other people. It was a moment that would not be forgotten, but relegated to a place of unimportance, at least for now.

Michael made his word bond and before the night was over took his daughter to get ice cream. Ivy wouldn't fully process what she saw for years to come. If there were questions in her mind, she wouldn't be able to articulate them for some time. Ivy was just glad when her father put her back in the car and the two made their way to the ice cream stand. She would have liked to eat the ice cream in the brightly colored shop with the smell of sweetness lingering in the air. She would have liked to sit in the white chairs with the heart shaped rod iron back and kick her legs slightly as she ate her chocolate chip ice cream. Ivy would have loved to sit across the table from her dad, watch him eat his favorite mint ice cream way too fast while getting little bits of light green confection in his neatly trimmed mustache. Instead, Ivy was content to sit in the back seat of her father's Cadillac Seville and eat her ice cream cone, watching her father through the rear-view mirror eat his. Her mother would fuss when she got home about the mess she made of her pink and purple, polka dot shirt but Geneva's fussing would be short lived. She too was just glad the two had the chance to spend time together, father and daughter.

Ivy would see the boys again, the woman too. She would also see another woman with another boy that called her dad, dad. Ivy's words and thoughts at nine were very different than her words and thoughts at five. Between the ages of five and nine, she would not just be introduced to these people but they would have names, they would be her brothers, they would play together, their mother's would be nice to her and take care of her when they were all together. It wasn't uncommon for Ivy to go to either of her brother's houses on a weekend when she spent time with her father.

One evening, while Geneva brushed and braided Ivy's hair, Ivy raised the question.

"Mama," Ivy began.

"Hold still, Ivy," Geneva replied as her daughter sat on the floor between her legs. Geneva continued to oil and brush her daughter's hair. For Geneva, this was one of her favorites; spending quality time with Ivy doing girl stuff. Of course, it was no picnic for Ivy who winced and ducked as her mother worked through her thick, shoulder length hair; brushing it with a heavy hand and braiding it so tight Ivy's head would hurt through the night into the morning.

"How come my brothers never come here to play?"

Ivy's question was innocent enough. The brush in Geneva's hand paused slightly as the painful question registered in her spirit. There was confirmation there, but no surprise. Geneva suspected for a long time there was someone else; another, others that shared her husband's affections. Michael was a charismatic and the ultimate charmer. He was not one to deny himself of the things he wanted. Geneva knew that included other women. Geneva knew there were other children too. She knew about the first and the third ones. At one point, she questioned her husband about the other people in his life, the other families. Michael made no excuses. He confirmed there were others. But they were not his wife. Geneva was his wife and Ivy was his daughter. Geneva shed quiet tears as her husband matter of factly told her of the other parts of his life, without apology. He expected acceptance from Geneva. He did promise her that unless she chose to, she would never have to see those other people. He would not flaunt the women or his other children in her face. It hurt, but Geneva accepted it. What real choice did she have? She just never thought this was something she would have to explain to her daughter.

"You've met the boys," Geneva inquired continuing to absentmindedly brush her daughter's hair.

"Yeah, we play together sometimes at their mothers' houses."

Ivy didn't recognize the hesitancy in her mother's brush strokes. She hadn't turned around to see the pain etched in her mother's face.

"Are the boys nice to you?"

"Yeah, most of the time," Ivy began.

"Most of the time?" The protective mother bear instinct rose slightly in Geneva.

"Little Michael is nice and so is Tommy, but Roderick likes to pull my hair," Ivy explained.

Geneva knew that Michael and Thomas belonged to Cheryl; the first 'girlfriend' she became aware of. Roderick must belong to Odessa, 'the second'. There was some relief as Geneva realized it was merely childhood antics and her baby wasn't being seriously hurt by the boys. Geneva took the opportunity to inquire further. Maybe she could get answers, insight from her daughter that Michael would never provide.

"Are the boys' mommies nice to you?"

"Mmmhmm," Ivy continued without the briefest delay. "Auntie O let me help her bake cookies one day. I got to lick the spoon and everything!"

Auntie O, Geneva thought to herself. Hmph is what rose up in her spirit, but she didn't say anything. She listened as Ivy continued.

"Auntie Cheryl is nice too. She lets me play in her makeup and stuff."

Hearing that her daughter had a relationship, any kind of relationship with those other women was heart wrenching for Geneva. She didn't refer to them as Ms. or some other formal salutation. Ivy called them Aunt. Maybe that was the instruction given to them by her father or the other two women. Maybe it was something Ivy came to on her own. Whatever it was, Ivy's knowledge of them and spending time with them sickened Geneva.

"Mama, you didn't answer my question," Ivy said as she bumped against her mother's leg trying to get her attention. Geneva zoned out in her own tortured thoughts, no longer attending to her daughter or her hair.

"I'm sorry, baby girl, what was the question again," Geneva asked stroking her daughter's hair.

"When can the boys come over here and play?"

"I don't know, Ivy, we'll see…" The question hurt the second time as much as it did the first. Geneva had no intention of allowing "the boys" or their wretched mothers into her home; the home for her family. She said what she said to appease her daughter and to deflect the question.

Chapter Two

… Ivy Renee Francis Sims…

Twelve-year-old Ivy stormed into the house after school. Her friends from the neighborhood were already gathering outside and she wanted to be a part of it.

"Hey, ma," Ivy called. "I'm going back outside."

"Hold on one minute, young lady," Geneva stated coming out of the kitchen wiping her hands on a dish towel.

Ivy, with her hand on the doorknob, stopped and turned to face her mother.

"I received a call from your teacher today, Ivy," Geneva began as she sat on the arm of the couch. "Anything you care to share?"

"About what?" Ivy quipped placing her free hand on her narrow hip. She tightened her dark brown, almond shaped eyes and glared at her mother.

"About the fact that you were caught skipping class today, Missy and the fact that your grades have been slipping."

Ivy figured before she got home the school would call. That's why she tried to get out of the door before her mother could accost her.

"What difference does it make?"

"Excuse me?" Geneva replied, standing up and walking over to where her daughter stood. "It makes a lot of difference. You know how much we value education in this household. Education is your ticket to making a way for yourself. That's the difference!"

"It didn't do nothin' for you..." Ivy mumbled under her breath just loud enough for her mother to hear.

Geneva was taken aback. The relationship between the two had been strained for a while now. Geneva attributed it to Ivy being a teenager and having the typical teenage attitude. But this was downright disrespectful.

"What did you say, young lady?" Geneva spoke softly, but her words were laden with intensity. It didn't seem to matter to Ivy.

"I said, it didn't do nothin' for you!" Ivy didn't back down. Instead she closed the distance even further between herself and her mother.

"All the education you got really paid off, huh? You graduated from high school and even went to college didn't you, ma? And what way did you make with all that education? Hmph... It takes a lot of smarts to cook and clean and take care of a man don't it, mama?"

"You betta watch your mouth, Ivy Renee Francis," Geneva charged back.

"I don't even know why he keeps you around... Auntie O and Auntie Cheryl taking your place anyway..."

Before Geneva could stop herself, she slapped Ivy with an open hand across the face. Her reaction shocked her as much as it did Ivy. Geneva covered her mouth in disbelief and Ivy covered her stinging face in greater disbelief.

Ivy crumpled to the floor. Geneva moved quickly to her daughter who brushed her away.

"How could you let him treat you like that," Ivy wailed, as much from the hurt of her face as the hurt from her heart. She didn't wait for a response.

"All these years, mama, he's had other women, other kids and what do you do about it? Everybody know daddy got other women... whole other family's right outside this door. They're laughing at you, behind your back. Did you know that? At first I tried to defend you, stand up for you, but I can't even do that no more 'cause you ain't standing up for yourself! Nothing! You just keep taking care of him and letting him do whatever he wants to... If that's what being educated gets you, then I don't want it. I don't want to be nothin' like you."

Getting up from the floor, Ivy pushed past her mother and bolted for her bedroom slamming the door behind her. She loved her mother, but she lost respect for her a long time ago.

Geneva slumped to the floor, stunned from the stinging words her daughter spoke. All this time Geneva thought she was doing the right thing; doing whatever it took to keep her family together. Geneva wanted to run behind her daughter, to explain why she did what she did and why every sacrifice was worth it. Now Geneva realized there was a cost she never factored in.

9:30 p.m.

That was the time the text message read that both Brock and Parker received. They were dutiful in their response, meeting up within minutes of each other outside Ivy's building. Neither dared to be late. They both understood and respected Ivy's utter intolerance for tardiness. Brock checked his watch. It was 9:28. It wasn't quite time to buzz up either. Although Parker and Brock were in intimate situations on a number of occasions, they really didn't know each other. Their encounters were focused solely on Ivy. There had been no occasion for casual conversation. The two stood there awkwardly waiting for time to pass. The last two minutes seemed to take forever. Parker shifted her weight from one foot and then the other pretending to be interested in something on her cell phone. Brock repeatedly checked his watch as he observed the slow-moving traffic going by.

At precisely 9:30 p.m. Brock rang the buzzer. There was a slight delay before Ivy responded and buzzed the two upstairs. Brock, being the perfect gentleman, opened the door and allowed Parker to walk in front of him. Watching her walk up the stairs, he took note of why Ivy invited her to the party. She was shapely in all the places that mattered most with a tight waist and a serious apple bottom. He decided at that moment, if given the opportunity, he would take full advantage of what Parker had to offer.

The two arrived at Ivy's apartment and Parker knocked on the door. There was another smile shared between the two as they waited for Ivy to invite them in. When she opened the door, all attention turned in her direction. Ivy stood, all 5'9, completely naked with the exception of the open toed four inch slippers that accentuated her shapely legs. Her ebony skin glimmered as if she'd bathed in sunshine and its glowing remnants were absorbed into her very essence. Stepping through the threshold, Parker greeted Ivy warmly with a kiss. Brock followed suit and behind him, Ivy closed the door.

Ivy wasn't one for meaningless conversation. As a matter of fact, there was little conversation to be had. Everyone knew their purpose for being there so there was no small talk. Ivy led the trio into the bedroom.

"Undress..." a simple instruction given by Ivy that was quickly followed.

Seeing Ivy in her divine glory and watching Parker as she undressed gave Brock an instant hard on. Brock was not the least bit surprised; however, when Ivy summoned Parker and relegated him to the couch adjacent to her king-sized bed.

Parker eagerly joined Ivy on the bed and wasted no time in hungrily kissing Ivy's luscious lips. Parker had been completely infatuated with Ivy since their first encounter. Parker considered herself heterosexual as before Ivy, she'd never been with another woman. Her only sexual experience had been with men. When she met Ivy, quite by happenstance, she was immediately smitten with her presence. Yes, she thought Ivy was physically very attractive for a woman, but there was something about Ivy that Parker found alluring. The two met in a business context. Ivy was the marketing consultant on a project for the merchandising firm Parker worked for. Ivy made a presentation to the heads of the company. Parker couldn't take her eyes off Ivy. She was smart, confident, sassy when she needed to be and very forthright. Ivy had the company heads eating out of her hands midway through the presentation and they signed off on a quarter of a million-dollar consulting deal that afternoon. Ivy took it in stride as if having powerful people cowtow to her was no big deal.

After the meeting, Parker made it her business to share with Ivy how impressed she was with Ivy's business acumen. Being up close and in Ivy's personal space gave Parker butterflies; a feeling she hadn't experienced in quite a while. She was enamored with Ivy. Ivy being astute, invited Parker to have drinks following the meeting and the rest, shall we say was history. That first night, it was just the two of them. Ivy seduced Parker without ever taking her clothes off. Later that evening when they did become physical, all thoughts of Parker's sexual orientation went out the window. She had to have Ivy; the woman was just intoxicating.

It was only after they had a few encounters did Ivy lay down the rules for Parker. By this point, Parker would have agreed to anything Ivy said. She had to be with her. Ivy was her forbidden fruit.

After eight months, Parker still felt the same way. For Parker, Ivy made the air in the room thin; making it hard to breath, keeping her lightheaded. Parker basked in Ivy's presence, her jewel already pulsating from the thought of what was to come. Ivy leaned her back against the black leather, button tufted headboard and opened her legs revealing her sweet spot. Parker continued to kiss Ivy and nibble her ears then her neck as her fingers found Ivy's tenderness. Parker inserted one finger then two, thrusting slowly in and out. Parker's hips gyrated with each thrust as she continued to crest toward her first orgasm. Needing some relief, Parker used her free hand to massage her own pearl as she continued to languish inside Ivy.

Turned on by the two women, Brock watched from the couch. Ivy watched him watching them. Brock stroked his shaft and Ivy shook her head no. His eyes pleaded with hers as he too needed relief from the tension building in his nine-inch pole. Again, Ivy's nonverbal was clear. He was to watch and watch only, until otherwise instructed. And he would do what he was instructed to do despite his discomfort and desire.

Parker removed her fingers from Ivy's sweet spot and licked the succulent nectar from each one. She had to have more. She wanted to taste more of the woman she craved. Parker left a trail of long, deep kisses down Ivy's chest and belly as she made her way to the treasure. Parker breathed in deeply, taking Ivy's scent deep into her nostrils. She admired the beauty of Ivy's cut and smiled up at Ivy as she began to laden Ivy's inner thighs with kisses and nibbles. Parker pushed her tongue past the folds of Ivy's jewel box and found the pearl. Initially, softly then with more intensity, Parker sucked Ivy. Ivy's eyes never left Brock as she placed one hand to the back of Parker's head; encouraging her to lick deeper and suck harder. Parker continued to finger herself in rhythm with the loving she shared with Ivy. Parker moaned inside Ivy and was blessed with hot liquid nectar which Parker eagerly consumed.

Brock could barely contain himself; the visual and auditory stimulation caused his heart to beat faster and his dick to become rock hard. Ivy knew exactly what she was doing by making him wait. When she finally called for Brock with a simple gesture of her hand, he smiled and crossed the room to join in. Ivy kept the condoms in the nightstand by the bed. Brock opened the drawer to get one. Before he put it on, Ivy reached out and stroked Brock's manhood. He allowed his head to drop back between his shoulders as he relished her touch. Brock groaned deeply as Ivy massaged his engorged cock. Ivy took her free hand and lifted Parker from her and directed her to Brock's throbbing member.

"Aw shit," Brock exclaimed as Parker wrapped her luscious lips around him. Again, between these two, no words were spoken. It wasn't necessary. Brock was sexy as hell and Parker had no qualms about being with him, especially if it pleased Ivy. Wrapping both her hands around his pole, Parker sucked slow and deep. Brock's cock grazed the back of her throat. His hips tightened and flexed with every thrust as he slowly gyrated in her wanton mouth. Ivy made her way off the bed. Reaching into another side table drawer, she brought out her toy, a double headed steel strap-on dildo. She made her way to the side of the bed where Brock stood. He reached down and kissed her intensely. Brock loved Ivy's lips and locked into an enthralling kiss for as long as she would allow.

When the two separated, Ivy strapped up. Parker's eyes gleamed as she saw the toy. She knew exactly what that meant. She couldn't wait to have Ivy fuck her. Parker quickened her pace, taking Brock in deeper and faster. She tasted the gism from his tip and licked it satisfyingly. Once commanded, Parker released Brock and changed her position on the bed, getting on all fours. Ivy positioned herself between a standing Brock and a lying Parker. Brock busied himself with putting on a condom; never taking his eyes off the two women in front of him. Ivy inserted the slightly shorter steel tip into Parker's v-spot getting it moist. Easing out, Ivy cuffed Parker's ass and spread her cheeks, sliding one tip into her ass and the other in Parker's puss. With the dual penetration, squeals oozed from Parker's lips.

With her heels on, Ivy was just about the right height. All it took was for her to bend forward slightly so Brock could implant himself in her jewel box. Brock held Ivy's waist. Ivy did the same with Parker. When he thrust forward, the force caused a thrusting from Ivy to Parker. The grind was methodical, deep and penetrating; each body moving in sync with the next. Moans of exhilaration escaped lips as the threesome moved in rhythmic syncopation. Ivy lifted one leg and rested it on the bed causing new angles and new tensions to be formed. Brock did everything he could to hold on to his nut. He didn't want the magic to stop, but it was getting harder and harder to keep from cumming. As the pace increased, Brock's balls slapped against Ivy's ass as her makeshift cocks found deeper realms to explore inside Parker.

"Damn, baby... I can't hold it!" Brock's body spasmed as the gism in his manhood rose.

"Oh, god, Ivy, fuck me, please don't stop, please," Parker begged as she too brimmed on the edge of exploding.

Brock felt new warmth welcoming his deep thrusts. It was enough to cause his mind to temporarily go blank. There was a collective crescendo; voices raised, gyrations reaching a fevered pitch and then communal climax... each person lost themselves in the sensations caused by the other.

"Damn, Ivy... I love you..."

Parker's voice was raspy and breathy from exhilaration. Instantly, Parker knew she committed the ultimate sin. Her eyes were wide as she turned to look in Ivy's direction; unable to fully do so because of their entanglement. Parker regretted her outburst. She knew her transgression was unforgiveable.

With those words, it was as if the wind behind a bold sail immediately vanished. Those were forbidden words and a definite breech of the rules. Ivy kept a cool head. There would be no outburst, no scolding. Brock eased himself from Ivy fully aware of Parker's violation. Ivy allowed Parker to disengage herself from the toy. As Ivy moved away from the bed unstrapping the harness, she stopped briefly and turned to her two lovers.

"Brock, you stay. Parker, leave... and don't come back."

Brock dutifully followed Ivy into the adjoining master bath as Parker pulled herself together and gathered her things. Parker was devastated; chastising herself without words because she knew she fucked up. Ivy wasn't down for that love shit, even if it was a mistake. Now she had to pay. Parker wanted to explain, to let Ivy know she was just caught up in the moment and she didn't mean it. Well, she did mean it... but none of that mattered now, did it? Parker looked longingly in Ivy's direction as the two disappeared behind the closed door. She would let herself out.

Chapter Three

… I am my father's daughter…

"Ivy Renee Frances Sims, this is the last time I'm going to tell you to get up. The bus will be here any minute."

That was Ivy's mother's third attempt at rousting her 14-year-old daughter out of bed. But Ivy was still slow to move. It had been a long night in the Frances home; not unlike many other nights before, but long nonetheless. When Ivy finally got up, dressed and ready for school, she dragged her feet as she made her way to the kitchen.

"It's about time, young lady," her mom chided.

"Whateva..." Ivy mumbled under her breath just loud enough for her mother to hear. Ivy flopped down in the kitchen chair and placed both elbows on the table; something she knew got under her mother's skin.

Ivy's mother heard her smart aleck reply, but didn't respond. For one, she was too tired from the night before. Two, it didn't matter any way. She lost control of Ivy a long time ago and Geneva Sims was too tired to fight to get her back. She was too tired of fighting her husband, Michael.

Well, fighting wasn't really the word. It was more like ducking and dodging and trying to protect herself from his latest anger outburst.

Geneva closed the refrigerator and placed the bowl of cereal and carton of milk on the table in front of Ivy. Long ago she stopped pouring milk on her daughter's cereal. For some reason, she could never get the amount right. One day it was too much, the next not enough. She didn't want to argue, so she let Ivy do it herself. It was better that way.

Geneva instinctively turned her head slightly so Ivy couldn't see the damage her father did to her face the night before. She tried to cover it with makeup, but this time the bruising around her eye and the cut on her upper lip were too dark and deep for the fair toned makeup to hide. Still, Geneva did her best to camouflage the evidence.

But Ivy saw her mother's face.

"...probably deserved it," she muttered grabbing the milk carton and pouring the milk; allowing the milk to crest and spill over the edge of the bowl. Ivy smirked.

"Oops...so sorry," she quipped as she slammed the carton down, harshly backed the chair from the table, and grabbed her backpack. Ivy didn't even look back as she made her way to the front door of the apartment, grabbed her keys and headed out the door. The sarcastic smile still remained as she slammed the door behind her.

Tears welled in Geneva's eyes as she watched her daughter leave. She allowed the bitter tears to spill over as she reached for the paper towels. Geneva cried quietly as she slowly wiped up the spilled milk. Picking up the bowl from the table, her unsteady hand caused milk to pour over the edge.

"UHHHHHH," she screamed turning on her heels and throwing the leaking bowl in the sink. Hot tears spilled effortlessly as Geneva gave voice to her frustration and pain. Her face still hurt, but she cried because of the pain in her chest. Her heart was broken.

"I'm so tired," Geneva cried through her sobs. Leaving the mess in the kitchen behind, Geneva absentmindedly grabbed a knife off the counter. She made her way to the only bathroom in the two-bedroom apartment. She pushed the door after her but it didn't close all the way. Geneva didn't bother to close it. What difference would it make? She plugged the tub and turned on the water. Living on the fifth floor of the building, sometimes it took a while for the water to get hot. Geneva didn't bother to check it. Dropping her faded pink robe to the linoleum floor, Geneva stepped into the old, claw foot bath tub with the knife still in her hand. She barely noted the lukewarm water temperature as she sat down.

There were aches and pains from the night before; many aches and pains from many of such nights all dulled by Geneva's devotion to her husband for the sake of her daughter. All of Geneva's pains were not physical ones. Michael wasn't always physically aggressive. But his words cut deep. His dismissal of her wounded Geneva's soul. The relegated position she allowed herself to be in because of who she was to him, tore at the fabric of her very nature. Although painful, sometimes the physical blows didn't hurt quite as much.

She never wanted Ivy to be without a father figure. The absence of her own played a significant part in why Geneva chose the kind of man she chose as her life mate. Was she cognizant of the link between an absent father and her current husband? Most likely, no. Geneva didn't fancy herself too philosophical. For all practical purposes, Geneva was a small-town girl from Mixonville, Alabama, with dreams of a husband, two children and a home of her own complete with a white picket fence.

That's not quite what Geneva got, however. She left her small town to move to the big city for better opportunities. At least that's what her mother wanted for her.; an opportunity to do more with her life than maybe she had. Geneva did as her mother requested and moved to Atlanta. She attended Morris Brown College and majored in education. Geneva was bright and a good student. At times, the big city was overwhelming; so many people, so many new experiences. Then, she met Michael Frances Sims.

He wasn't a student, but worked near the city-based campus. Their meeting was by happenstance, but Geneva was immediately smitten by him. Michael was a bit older, charming and take charge. He was smart, but not in a conventional way. He had been around and knew things. Geneva, felt she could learn a lot from him; more than what books could ever teach her. Michael's confidence made Geneva feel safe. He helped her navigate in a city that was still foreign to her. Michael's attention to her made her feel secure. It wasn't long before she began to follow her own dream and abandon that of her mother.

Geneva was so in love with Michael. He, in turn, seemed to be very much in love with her. He was a man, he had his quirks, but Geneva was okay with that. Michael promised to love her and take care of her. In the beginning, he did just that. She never paid much attention to the isolation, she was a loner anyway. Geneva didn't really concern herself with other women looking at her man or him giving other women a smile and a glance. As long as he came home to her, she wasn't bothered. He was an attractive man so it was only natural for other women to notice how handsome her husband was. That was the magical word for Geneva, husband. So, the rumors about Michael having another woman and then other women and another child and then other children were not rumors Geneva heard. If and when she did, she never concerned herself with them. She had her family; her husband and her daughter.

It was only when one of the women, Cheryl, brought the outside world to Geneva's front door. Geneva was at home, as usual, taking care of her wifely and motherly duties; cleaning house, doing laundry, making dinner. The doorbell rang. It was too early to be Michael and he wouldn't ring the bell because he had a key. It wouldn't be Ivy. It wasn't time for her to be out of school. Needless to say, Geneva answered the door, very unassumingly. When she opened the door, she was greeted by a woman who was pretty and very much pregnant.

"May I help you," Geneva asked looking the young woman up and down.

"You must be her," the woman responded. Her pretty face was not so pretty because of the sneer across her lips and the nasty in her voice.

"I'm not sure who the 'her' is you are looking for," Geneva replied. Something in her gut told her this wasn't an accidental encounter, but she wouldn't give the woman at the door the benefit of her knowing. "You must have the wrong address." Geneva was fully prepared to close the door and moved in that direction when the young lady stopped the closing door with an extended hand.

"No, this is the right address," the young lady continued. Geneva was tolerant of the woman's disrespectful tone and harsh intent, but she wasn't going to abide too much more of it.

"Who exactly are you looking for?" Geneva's hand was on her hip and now the tone in her voice mimicked that of this unwanted guest.

"Michael, Michael Francis Sims is who I'm looking for," the young lady fired back. She made sure to rub her protruding belly as she spoke.

"And what business do you have with Mr. Michael Francis Sims?"

"I need to talk to him about our situation," she said rubbing her stomach again for effect.

Geneva didn't immediately respond. To allow her real emotions to show in the moment would be counterproductive.

"And your name is," Geneva inquired keeping a cool head even though there was a deep and abiding sting to her heart with the prospect of what this woman proposed.

"I'm Cheryl, Cheryl Blackmon."

"Well, Cheryl Blackmon, I'm Mrs. Michael Francis Sims," Geneva retorted with a matter of fact air. "I'm his wife, the woman he chose to marry. You have no business with my husband that matters."

41

With that pronouncement, Geneva closed the door. She had to. She couldn't hold her peace any longer. Cheryl, however, didn't go away quietly into that good night. She banged on the door; declaring that she did indeed have business with Michael and this was not the end of it. Geneva leaned against the door. When Cheryl beat on the door, Geneva felt it on the other side; the shaking of the wood between her and the ugly side of her husband.

Geneva told Michael about her encounter over dinner that evening. Michael didn't deny knowing Cheryl or the fact she very well may be pregnant with his child. He apologized to Geneva because his promise to her had been broken. His business in the streets was never supposed to breech the sanctity of their home and it had. For that, Michael was indeed sorry. He promised Geneva it would never happen again and it didn't. Geneva never knew what Michael said to that other woman or women that followed, but Michael's promise to her stayed true.

But none of that seemed to matter much as Geneva leaned her head back on the rim of the tub and allowed the remaining few soulful tears to fall. That was one promise he kept. There were so many others that were broken. Both hands lay limply by her side underwater. The kitchen knife, still in her left hand, rested in the tepid water.

"I'm so tired..."

The only noise heard in the small bathroom was the incessantly slow drip of the faucet and a deep exhale from Geneva.

"Pass me not..." Geneva's voice was raspy. This was her favorite hymn from when she was a little girl in church. "...oh gentle Savior..."

She placed her right wrist on the edge of the tub and lifted the knife from the water. So many things that happened in her life were intentional. Geneva married the man she loved intentionally. She gave birth to a beautiful little girl after the two agreed it was time to start a family... intentional.

"...hear my humble cry..."

Geneva made a home for her small family. She was a dutiful wife and mother... intentional. Geneva lived her lifelong dream, intentionally. Michael had other women, other children, other families. That too was intentional. He had a short fuse and a quick tongue, intentional. His fist was quick when he felt it necessary; again intentional...

The deep and jagged cut Geneva made to one wrist and then the other was also intentional.

"...while on others though art calling..."

Geneva continued to sing the song that soothed her heart. The words were harder to come by as the life blood began to pour from her veins. The warmth of the tears spilling on Geneva's cheeks matched the warmth of the blood being expelled from her body.

"...Savior, do not pass me by..."

It was barely a whisper, but there was peace... calm, for Geneva in the words. The contradiction of Geneva's actions and her words were of little relevance.

Geneva lay her head back against the rim of the tub as the lukewarm water turned from clear to a darkly tinged pink. The knife dropped to the linoleum floor leaving drops of bright red blood on the black and white tiles.

"I'm... so... ti-..."

Chapter Four

... it's so hard to say good-bye...

She knew she was supposed to just go away, never see Ivy again, but Parker just couldn't let it go. Once you had a little bit of Ivy, you wanted more, you desired more, you needed more. Parker was in a desperate state of need. She had to take a chance at getting back into Ivy's life, if only for a little while.

It was a risk, true enough, but one Parker was more than willing to take. Showing up to Ivy's place with a stranger? Yeah, big risk. But she did.

There was no response to the initial ringing of the buzzer. Parker's hopes of redemption were almost dashed as she looked at her friend Assent disappointedly. Before turning to walk away, Parker opted to ring the buzzer one more time, just in case.

"Yes," the voice came over the speaker. It was Ivy. Parker was relieved. But now the nerves kicked in. She soldiered on.

"It's me, Parker."

There was silence. The low hum from the line was the only thing that could be heard. That's not what Parker hoped for.

"Please, Ivy," Parker continued not caring how desperate she sounded in front of Assent. "I need to see you."

Again, silence. Parker's disappointment and desperation increased simultaneously.

And then the line cracked.

"Why?"

Parker didn't have to consider the question. She leaned against the brick wall that contained the mechanism that connected her to her fix. The moment although public was an intimate one. Parker smiled as she spoke sweetly into the intercom.

"Because…"

Ivy knew what kind of effect she had on people. Ivy knew the impact she had on Parker. No further words were necessary.

She did make her wait a few moments before she buzzed her up. Maybe Ivy felt benevolent. Maybe she was bored. Whatever the reason, she entertained Parker's request as long as it suited her.

Grabbing Assent's hand, Parker led her enticement through the door and to the elevator. She didn't try to hide the broad smile she wore. All she needed was a chance, one chance to get back into Ivy's good graces. Ivy was giving her that chance. Parker told Assent of the importance of this meeting. Assent was a willing participant, curious about this Ivy Parker couldn't stop obsessing over. When the elevator reached Ivy's floor, there was a skip of Parker's heart. The two moved quickly down the hallway and stood in front of Ivy's door.

To say she waited with baited breath for the heavy steel and dark wood door to open was an understatement. Parker practically danced in the hallway with anticipation. When she heard the door's lock click, signaling release, Parker breathed in deeply. She had to calm herself or she would be summarily dismissed by the one she desired. She couldn't afford to be anxious. That was a turn off for Ivy.

The door swung open. Parker's heart skipped two beats; one because she was nervously excited, the second because Ivy was stunning.

There was a moment of assessment. Ivy looked passed Parker to the one who stood slightly behind her. Ivy took in the woman's chocolate mocha skin, tall frame, slender build and deep dark eyes. The bait's messy, natural hair said to Ivy she was confident in her own skin. She liked the fact that this woman didn't drop her gaze when their eyes met. Ivy was intrigued.

"Is she for me?" Ivy asked; her face still not giving away her interest.

"Yes," Parker submitted, hoping her gift was acceptable.

After a few seconds, and another full body view of Parker's gift, Ivy stepped to the side allowing them in.

Parker was absolutely relieved. Assent, seeing Ivy for herself, was equally enticed. The two eagerly followed Ivy into her expansive living space. There was no offering to sit or a suggestion of something to drink. Ivy headed straight for the master bedroom. There was no hesitation in either of her guests' step.

Ivy stopped in front of her bed and turned to face Parker and her gift. She allowed the black lace sheath to fall from her curvy body. Ivy kept her eyes on her present. When she smiled, Ivy did too. Parker was the first to move, interpreting Ivy's disrobing as an invitation. Ivy put up her hand, halting Parker in motion.

"If she's for me, then give her to me."

It took Parker a minute to understand Ivy's instruction. She knew she better get it quick or her grateful entry would be another decisive dismissal. Assent understood though, and turned to Parker to help her out. Assent began to unbutton her own blouse, maintaining eye contact with Parker trying to coax her without words. It felt that if either of them spoke a cardinal rule would be broken and Assent didn't want to break the rules before she had the chance for an Ivy experience. Assent took a step in Parker's direction, moving to the next button. Parker smiled when she realized what she needed to do and took over unbuttoning and then removing Assent's blouse. Assent was not one for the restraints ascribed to women. When Parker removed her top, Ivy was pleased to see perky, full breasts with plump nipples. Instinctively she began to massage her own breasts as she continued to eye Assent's.

Feeling a penetrating gaze, Assent turned to face Ivy as Parker continued to undress her. There was a magnetic charge between the two women. Ivy's eyes were simultaneously inviting and devouring. Assent wanted to drop her gaze because of the intensity, but found the magnetism much too strong, so she didn't... Between her thighs heat grew... Parker was dutiful in disrobing Assent. When she was done, she gently grabbed Assent by the waist and turned her body to face Ivy. Parker noticed the two had already connected. Ivy looked at Assent in a way she never regarded Parker. There was a tinge; a moment of second guessing for Parker.

Confirmation would soon follow as Assent closed the distance between herself and Ivy. The two stood close enough to kiss, but physical touch was not required for the heat between Assent's thighs to rage. Ivy was still cool though. She knew desire when she saw it. The only decision she needed to make was whether she would make Parker watch the unfolding. Assent couldn't stand being that close without touching the darkness of Ivy's skin. She zoned in on Ivy's luscious lips and she extended herself to kiss her. But that was not to be. Ivy turned away from her, stopped Assent and moved toward the bed. Parker was not to be dissuaded nor did she intend to be left out. She began to undress as she observed Ivy sitting on the edge of the bed with Assent standing in front of her.

Ivy cupped Assent's mocha breast with her hands and began to slowly suck on the pert nipple. And there it was, the touch that Assent knew she desired. The moan that emerged from Assent's lips was inescapable as instant electricity coursed through her body. The touch was everything Parker said it would be and so much more. Assent was unsure as to whether she could reciprocate with a touch to Ivy so she didn't; instead making herself keep her hands to her sides and accepting Ivy's seduction. Ivy lingered there, suckling, as if there were nourishment to be drawn from Assent's bosom.

Having given both breasts equal attention, Ivy traced Assent's silhouette with her finger appreciating every inch, every curve.

"I like her... I think I'll keep her..." Ivy commented, directing her words to Parker but never taking her eyes off Assent's body.

Parker wasn't sure what to do. She was relieved her offering was accepted, but did that mean she was still not welcomed? Parker stood there in all her naked glory waiting on a signal, some kind of sign from Ivy. Parker desperately wanted to stay, to be back in the fold. Maybe Assent was too nice of a gift?

"May I," Assent asked cautiously.

Ivy looked up and their eyes locked. She smiled coolly before responding.

"Yes, you may."

And with that, Assent was invited in. She dropped to her knees and again attempted to kiss Ivy. This time she was allowed. The kiss was tentative at first. Assent wanted to taste her so she didn't rush. And then she kissed her deeply; their tongues intertwining, their lips entangled. Assent felt pulsations in her puss that needed to be attended to but she was willing to let things unfold at the pace Ivy dictated.

As their lips separated, Assent gently pressed against Ivy's legs, encouraging them to open. There was no resistance from Ivy when Assent kissed her inner thighs and worked her way to Ivy's jewel. She explored Ivy, kissing and licking her outer folds and then inserting her tongue into Ivy's warmth. Assent appreciated the way she smelled. She loved the way Ivy tasted. Every drop of nectar that oozed from Ivy's hot box, Assent accepted; licking and sucking on Ivy's swollen pearl. Ivy palmed the back of Assent's head pushing her further into her folds. Ivy looked at Parker. Parker squirmed, licking her lips as though she too could remember the way Ivy tasted.

But there was no invitation. Parker was not welcomed. Her gift was accepted, but she wasn't. As Assent and Ivy continued to explore the newness of each other, all Parker could do was stand idly by. It seemed neither of them remembered Parker was even there. They noticed less when she left.

Ivy thought very little of her mom, as Ivy went about her day at school. Her only hope was that her father would be there when she got home. Things were always better when her dad was home. He kept things in order and to him, Ivy could do no wrong. Maybe that was his way of assuaging his own guilt for the other women and children he had that Ivy learned about in a not so delicate way. Nonetheless, he was her father, hers...

The bus ride home was always an adventure. Ivy was popular with the kids so the ride was always a good time. Upon arriving home, she didn't see her father's car so she hung outside with some friends, despite the repeated warnings from her mother that she needed to come in the house first to let mom know she was home. When Ivy's friends were required to go home, she had no choice but to do so as well. Begrudgingly, she made her way to their apartment, put her key in the door, and entered. She didn't call out for her mother. Ivy really didn't care if she saw her or not. More than that, her mother was always at home. Where else would she be? She was sort of like a recluse, no work, no friends, no nothing.

Ivy left her book bag and shoes at the door, went straight to her room and closed the door behind her. She called her father to see when he would be home, but he didn't answer. It was only after Ivy got hungry that she exited her room and headed for the kitchen. She hadn't paid attention to the fact that the apartment was unusually still or that her mother didn't call for her when she came in. Exiting her bedroom and heading toward the kitchen, Ivy noticed the bathroom door ajar. It was odd. Either the bathroom door was completely open when vacant or completely closed when occupied. Geneva had a thing about partially opened doors. Someone could be hiding behind them or something foolish like that. Retrieving a can of pop from the refrigerator, Ivy headed back to her room. In passing, she looked toward the bathroom door, this time digesting what she saw.

It was the red standing starkly against the black and white tiles that drew the young Ivy's attention. There was no reason for it to be there. Geneva kept a meticulously clean home. When she didn't, Michael quickly reminded her of it, usually with a tongue lashing and a back hand. Curious, Ivy walked to the bathroom door and slowly pushed it open. Time seemed to stand still as the door swung noisily on its hinges. She never noticed the whine of the door before... Ivy's eyes traveled from the red spots on the black and white tile, to the knife, to her mother's arm dangling over the rim of the tub, to Geneva's head lying back on the rim. Her skin was ashy like the color drained out. Her mother's eyes were open but unfocused. The bruising to her mother's face Ivy so decisively dismissed earlier in the day seemed darker and somehow more painful. For what seemed like the longest time, Ivy's feet wouldn't move. She couldn't make them move. She wasn't sure she wanted them to move.

Reluctantly, Ivy took a tender step forward and then another. That's when she saw her mother's naked body sitting in the dingy, red water. The can of pop fell haphazardly from Ivy's hand and it's only when her mind processed the sound of the can hitting the hard floor did she move quickly backwards, tripping over her own feet and landing on the floor. The pain she felt in her buttocks was nothing compared to what she saw. Quickly, Ivy scooted out of the bathroom, her eyes never leaving the site of her mother.

Heart racing, Ivy's first thought was her father. He would know what to do...

Ivy scrambled to her feet and raced to the phone in the kitchen, daring to take her eyes off her mother...

She dialed her father's number again; her feet dancing back and forth like she couldn't be still.

"Come on daddy, answer the phone... come on!!"

Again, the phone went to voice mail. When the beep came to leave a message, Ivy fell silent. What was she to say? "Oh, hey dad, mom is in the bathtub not moving. There's a knife on the floor and blood. Call me when you get a chance?" No, she couldn't find the words so Ivy hung up the phone.

Her next call was to 911.

When the operator answered, Ivy told her about the situation.

"Nine-one-one, what's your emergency?"

"It's my mother. She's dead."

The operator asked more probative questions, but Ivy's response remained flat, almost despondent.

"It's my mother. She's dead."

She wouldn't provide much more information than that. When asked was there anyone else at home was she at risk of being harmed, Ivy responded simply.

"No."

Because of technology, the dispatcher was able to track the location and dispatch emergency vehicles. She asked Ivy to remain on the line until help arrived. She did, but there was no further communication, at least not from Ivy.

"When the paramedics get to your house, you have to open the door, okay?"

Ivy nodded; not considering the dispatcher couldn't detect her nonverbal reply. It was only after the dispatcher repeated the question a second time, did Ivy say "yes". The line went silent again.

The dispatcher finally stopped trying to engage the caller in conversation. She was comfortable with the quiet only because the line stayed open and she could hear the young lady breathing. When she heard the knock on the door and the paramedics identify themselves, the dispatcher remained on the line until after she heard the young lady's final comment.

"They're here."

"Can you hand one of them the phone when they come in so I can be sure you're not alone?"

Ivy didn't reply, just did as the dispatcher requested and handed the first emergency worker who walked in the room the phone without giving any instruction. The worked unknowingly took the phone, confirmed their presence, and hung up.

"Where's your mom," an emergency worker asked.

Ivy pointed to the bathroom and the workers moved expeditiously as if there was a chance to save her. Ivy faded to the background.

Despite the obvious, the emergency workers did what procedurally they were required to do. After the photos were taken by the coroner's office, Geneva's body was lifted from the water. Ivy stepped as far back as she could when the workers who'd left moments before, returned with a gurney. The pronouncement was made and Geneva's lifeless body was placed on the crisp, white sheet. There was no reason to cover her body with clothing. The coroner would just undress her when she arrived at the morgue. As one of the emergency techs covered

Geneva's face with another white sheet, a female tech took note of the young lady leaning against the wall.

"Is there someone you can call," the EMT asked after making her way over to the young lady.

"I already called my dad," Ivy replied dryly. She didn't make eye contact with the EMT.

"Is he on his way? I would hate to leave you here alone," the EMT replied. Sure, the young lady looked old enough to be home alone, but given the circumstances, the EMT didn't think it best.

Ivy nodded her head in response to the question. It wasn't honest, but that didn't matter.

"Do you want one of us to stay until he arrives?"

Ivy shook her head. She just wanted them all to leave.

The EMT couldn't force the situation. She could place a call to Child Welfare Services and have a social worker dispatched to the home, but that would add insult to injury.

"Can you call him again to make sure he's on the way? I don't think you should be home alone," the EMT suggested.

Ivy was slow to move, but she knew if she didn't the lady would never leave her alone. Ivy walked to the kitchen and dialed her dad's number again.

Looking over her shoulder, she saw the EMT staring her down. Ivy turned her back and even though the phone went to voice mail, she pretended her father answered.

"Hey daddy, how long before you get here?" Ivy paused as if waiting for a reply. "Okay, hurry please." Ivy hung up the phone just as the EMT approached.

Before the EMT could ask, Ivy gave her the answer she knew the lady was looking for.

"He said he will be here in a few minutes." Ivy didn't wait for a reply. She returned to her spot on the wall and watched as the EMT returned to her duties. She wanted to press further, but trusted what the young lady said. The EMT couldn't afford to hold up the team because she felt uneasy.

As they wheeled her mother past her, time seemed to stand still for Ivy once again. The gurney moved so slowly in front of her, she could take in the peaks in the sheet from her mother's body and the slight lift in the white sheet where her mother's nose was. The female EMT looked at the young lady again and offered a sympathetic smile. No further words were exchanged between the two. When the door closed, Ivy's body slid down the wall. It wasn't a conscious thing. Her legs seemed to no longer be able to hold up her frail body. Ivy didn't scream. She didn't cry. Ivy sat in that spot staring blankly into the apartment. Her mind couldn't focus on anything. A few hours passed and she still hadn't moved. Her body needed to relieve itself, but Ivy refused to go in the bathroom. She willed the pressure pressing against her bladder away. She would never go in that bathroom again.

It was only when she heard the key turn in the lock that Ivy moved. She drew her feet in and stood up. When her father entered, their eyes met in the shadowy, dim light streaming through the window. Without words, Ivy moved toward her father and wrapped her arms around him. She buried her head in her father's chest. There were still no tears.

There was something wrong. Michael knew it. It wasn't uncommon for his daughter to call him, but she'd called him repeatedly without leaving a message. To see his beautiful little girl's face, it was confirmed something was terribly wrong. Ivy held him tightly; tighter than he could remember her holding him before. Stepping slightly back, Michael lifted his daughter's chin and their eyes met again.

"She's dead… she killed herself." Michael pulled his daughter back into his arms and held her. There was a break in his heart at that very moment. No matter how many other women there were in his life, Geneva was special, even if he never told her. She was his wife, the only one he ever married, the mother of his most precious child, and now she was gone.

He would take care of his daughter, he had no choice. Michael escorted Ivy to her room and helped her pack a few things. They moved in silence, each of them separately dealing with what happened. They didn't stay in the apartment long. Whatever else Ivy needed, Michael would provide it. For right now, he had to get her out of there. Once they got in the car, he would figure out where they would go. Michael didn't have a place of his own. Why should he? He had a home with his wife and a place to lay his head with the others when he chose to.

The two rode silently through the Atlanta streets. Michael pointed the car in the direction of downtown. Ivy stared straight ahead blankly. There were no tears. They would stay in a hotel for the night. He would have to make some moves and figure out the rest, but tonight, the hotel would do. Michael couldn't think too much past that. He would soon have to bury his wife.

Chapter Five

…love… a many splendid thing…

There was a point in Ivy's life where she thought she was in love. You know the kind of love we all dream about; that eternal, soul stirring love. She like many girls, like her mother, believed in true love, having a soul mate and living happily ever after. And despite some of the things Ivy saw growing up, there was a part of her that initially held out hope she would find the one she was meant to be with the rest of her life. Ivy thought she found that one. That one was Brock. Ivy met Brock at a time when she was open to possibilities. He represented everything she thought she ever wanted in a lifetime partner. Brock was smart, which was very important. Physically, Brock was a nod from the gods; his body articulated in such a way that to look at him made you smile. His skin was dark and smooth and his smile bright and enchanting. Brock was a beautiful man. He reminded Ivy of her father.

Even though Ivy wasn't convinced education was a means to success, she attended college because her father expected her to. Of course, he always encouraged her to hone her other skills, those that came naturally to any woman, but he also knew the importance of having those Roman papers that validated a person in societies' eyes. Michael wanted Ivy to be dually skilled. Her desire was to make her father proud.

For both Brock and Ivy, it didn't matter how they met. What was most important is that they met at all. There connection was instant, fiery, intense. Imagine that whole notion of seeing someone from across a crowded room and instantly being connected to them. Intensify that imagery by 1000%. There was a palatable current that passed between the two of them. To Ivy's liking, Brock didn't require a lot of conversation. There was a sense of knowing what the other wanted, needed; what their base animalistic desire was. More importantly, each was able to not only identify this primal instinct, but act unprovoked; driving the other to an even greater level of emotional intensity.

The feeling was addictive, and Ivy and Brock were both strung out. And that was fine, for a while. But Ivy was her father's child. And for reasons she never articulated but felt in her core, she was a rolling stone; never willing to stay in one spot too long for fear she would wither and die. Being that dependent on one person, being able to be hurt and broken by one person was unimaginable to Ivy. She saw firsthand what unwavering love and devotion could do to a person's soul. Ivy bore witness to what putting someone before yourself could do. She saw the end result of forgiving a person's transgressions because you just love them so much could do to a person. She saw what it did to her own mother. Ivy never forgot how loving one man ended her mother's life. She refused to allow that to be her story, no matter how deeply she felt for anyone.

So, Ivy did the opposite of what her mother did and mimicked her father whom she idolized. Ivy emotionally distanced herself from Brock, building a masonry wall around her heart and quieting her deepest feelings. She eliminated any feeling of vulnerability that may have been lingering in the shadows even if that's never what she overtly displayed to Brock. Ivy didn't allow herself to attach to people. She was careful when they tried to attach themselves to her. The entanglement with Brock, emotionally ended but physically intensified.

Ivy was good at the cutoff if she felt things were getting too intense, too clingy, bordering on something she might not be able to walk away from. She was good at the dismissal with anything and everything, anyone and everyone with the exception of Brock. Ivy, up until this point, had not completely shaken herself of him so she fucked him... but refused to feel. Brock was fine with that. He would rather have a piece of Ivy even if it was just scraps.

The long, black limousine pulled up to the house. Ivy stood at the window of Auntie Odessa's house. That's where she and her father ended up staying after a few nights in the hotel. Ivy and her dad consoled each other that first night; each experiencing the loss in their own way. Ivy wasn't a crier and her father was too much of a man to allow his daughter to see him in tears so the consoling was quiet. As close as Ivy and her father were, their time alone in that hotel room was awkward. They barely spoke. Ivy never doubted her father loved her, so their inability to connect in this moment didn't register for Ivy as a lack of love. Maybe her father was lost in his own thoughts. Maybe she was reliving the discovery of her mother's body. Neither could say for sure, but the silence between the two became deafening and Michael found respite in another woman's bed. Ivy didn't mind though. The distracting noise of other people was somehow comforting. Ivy watched from the window as the car parked near the curb; the yellow hazard lights blinking in syncopated rhythm. Ivy counted the tic tic of the blinks... tic... tic... tic...; her mind unfocused and her gaze blank.

"Boys, quit messing around and head for the car, the driver is here," Odessa called out from somewhere behind Ivy. She didn't turn around, just continued to count the tics. The boys brushed by Ivy, one mumbling under his breath, and made their way to the car. Odessa followed close behind, stopping to hug Ivy's shoulders.

"I'll see you in the car," Odessa said to Michael who was standing behind his daughter watching her. Ivy didn't realize her dad was there. She thought Odessa was speaking to her until she heard what sounded like a kiss and her father saying okay. Ivy didn't turn around and soon her father stood next to her at the window. The two stood there, neither of them speaking. Ivy continued to count the tics. After a few moments, her father spoke.

"Ready?"

Ivy nodded her head in the affirmative and the two exited the house. The driver opened the door for Ivy and her dad. Michael slid in beside Odessa and the boys were forced to get over so Ivy could get in. She sat by the window and looked out as the limousine made its way through the Atlanta streets to the funeral parlor where her mother's service would be held. There was some pressure from Geneva's family to have the service at the family's home church, but Michael was not much for religion. He was not much for Geneva's family either and much to their dismay, decided to have a small service at the local funeral home.

When the car pulled up to the funeral home, Odessa and her children filed out and went ahead. Ivy and her dad followed. Her mom's family was already gathered in the vestibule for the family procession into the parlor. As Ivy and her dad made their way to the front of the group, she could feel the eyes of the family on her and her dad. She felt the tension. She felt the judgment as none were unaware of the woman and her children who entered the parlor immediately before. Attendees opened the parlor doors and the family entered. There was somber funeral music playing in the background. Those who were gathered inside watched as the family filed in. The division in the parlor was obvious to any onlooker. Geneva's family sat on one side and nearly filled every row. Michael and Ivy sat on the front row on the other side. Odessa and her children, and Mama Cheryl and her son sat immediately behind. A few of Michael's friends from the neighborhood were there as well. The group barely filled three rows.

The music ended and a man Ivy didn't know stood before the gathering. He spoke very fondly of her mother and talked about the heaven she would surely enter because of the faithful life she led. There were 'amen's' coming from the other side of the parlor as those behind Ivy and her father sat quietly. After a few minutes, the man stopped talking and two men dressed in black suits walked to the front of the parlor. They stood in front of the casket, removed the spray of yellow flowers that lay on top and opened the coffin. Someone sitting on the other side started to cry as her mother's body came into view. Ivy's eyes stayed straight ahead, unfocused. She continued to count the tics even though the car was not physically there.

Ushers directed those in attendance to the front of the parlor so they could see Geneva one final time. Some stood quietly, others mourned loudly. Soon Odessa and Cheryl were paying their respects to Ivy's mom. The irony of that moment would come up for Ivy long after the funeral was over. When her father reached over and grabbed her hand, Ivy knew it was time to see her mom. A quiet hush fell over the parlor as Ivy and her dad walked up.

...tic...tic...

Ivy stood over her mother and after a few moments, looked down into the casket. The last time Ivy saw her mother was in a tub full of bloody water. This time, Ivy looked down at her mother, she barely recognized her. Geneva looked like herself, but she didn't look like herself. Her skin was pale and ashen. There were lots of makeup; something her mother would have never worn. To some, Geneva may have looked peaceful, but to Ivy her mother looked unreal…cold…dead…

Before leaving the casket, her dad leaned over and kissed her mother. Instead of returning to their seats, Ivy and her dad walked out of the parlor and to the limousine that awaited. Ivy heard a cadre of "I'm so sorry for your loss," from relatives she barely knew. Some even extended a hand to touch her as she passed.

The burial followed. The same man spoke a few words to those who gathered graveside and committed Geneva to the ground.

"From dust we were born and to dust we must return…"

The casket was lowered into the ground.

…tic…tic…

The family returned to the church for the repast. Ivy noted the mood was completely different. Folks who had been balling their eyes out, mourning the loss of their beloved Geneva were now stuffing their faces full of free food and laughing and talking. One thing that remained the same was the separation between the two sides of the family. Her mom's family sat together and Ivy sat with her dad and the few who gathered on his behalf. There was polite conversation, but nothing too intense. Odessa and

71

Cheryl respectively, attended to Ivy and her dad, making their plates and encouraging them to eat. Her mom's family stopped eating and laughing long enough to look disdainfully at the display of disrespect. The glares, stares and whispers from across the room couldn't be dismissed. The audacity of Michael and his women to show up like this was repeated loud enough for Ivy to hear. Odessa and Cheryl heard it too, but they heard it before. Each woman brushed it off and continued to cater to the man they loved.

The small talk at their table continued as if the snarky comments from the other side were never spoken. And before long it was over.

There was no further mention of Geneva.

Chapter Six

...break up... can we make up?

The buzzer sounded. It was early morning before the sun came up. The sky was still dark. There were a few cars moving on the street in front of the building, but there were few and far between. The buzzer sounded again, elongated like someone was laying on it. Assent roused.

"Did you hear that?"

Ivy was coming out of a deep sleep disturbed by the buzzer, but awoke because of Assent moving around in the bed.

The buzzer sounded again, this time it sounded like whoever was ringing it was tapping out a rhythm. Initially Ivy intended to ignore it. Maybe it was some drunk buzzing the wrong unit. But the repeated buzzing suggested they knew who they were there to see. Now she was irritated.

"Ignore it..." she replied, rolling Assent over and scooting up behind her melding their naked bodies together.

After a few moments, the buzzing stopped and Ivy prepared herself to nestle in for a few more hours of much needed rest.

And then the buzzer blared again, and again and again.

"...son of a bitch..."

Ivy was pissed. She threw the covers back and bounded from the bed. Whoever the fuck was leaning on her buzzer was about to get blasted. Assent sat up in the bed, her sleep disturbed as well. She covered her plump breasts with the silken duvet from the bed. Ivy didn't bother to put on any clothes. She fully intended to cuss whoever it was out over the buzzer and crawl back into her nice warm bed. The buzzer sounded again.

"What the fuck is your problem, dumb son of a bitch!" Ivy was seething and whoever was on the other end of her fiery words could definitely hear it in her voice.

"I need to talk to you," the person on the other end of the receiver quietly replied. Whoever it was had enough gumption to stay even after that tongue lashing.

"Who the fuck is this... *need to talk to me my ass, I need to be fucking sleep or fucking my girl but not fucking responding to no ignorant ass shit like this ... gottdamn sun ain't even up... need to talk to me my ass...*" Ivy said as much to herself as to the person she knew was listening.

There was a long pause and Ivy started to turn and walk away and then the voice box cracked again.

"It's me... Parker..."

This time the buzzer sounded from the other end and the door popped allowing Parker to enter the lobby. Parker was somewhat surprised Ivy let her in, but she was relieved and quickly made her way to Ivy's door. Parker rapped heavily on the door in quick succession.

When the door swung open, Parker was fully prepared to walk in but her forward movement was immediately halted as Ivy stood there in all of her divine nakedness. Parker was so taken aback by the

75

sight of Ivy, her mouth fell open slightly and she drunk Ivy in from head to toe.

"What the fuck is your problem?"

Uncharacteristically, Ivy didn't lower her voice. Her unit was the only one on her floor so there were no neighbors to overhear or disturb. Given Ivy's mood, she wouldn't have cared anyway. Ivy was the same pissed off as she was when Parker leaned on the buzzer the first time, maybe even more.

"Like I said, Ivy, I need to talk to you," Parker repeated still unable to look Ivy in the face as she was too busy staring at her old lover's body. That aggravated Ivy even more and she took her hand from her hip, grabbed Parker by the chin to make her focus and stepped forward leaving little distance between the two. Parker could feel Ivy's pert breasts brush against her slightly. She was instantly aroused.

"You must be out of your fuckin' mind. You come when I send for you... Did I fucking send for you, Parker? Did you get a text from me telling you to come? No, you didn't so I don't give a rat's ass how bad you feel you need to talk to me, you do not grace my doorstep unless I say you can... understood?"

Although the chastisement was curt, Parker smiled inside. How she missed Ivy's command. Ivy noticed the slight smile on Parker's face and considered slapping the shit out of her. Ivy wasn't flattered by Parker's lust filled gaze, not in the least. But Ivy was not prone to violence and decided instead to close the door and let Parker do what she needed to do without further disturbing her situation. But, before the door could completely close, Assent walked into the foyer.

"Everything okay, Ivy?"

Parker's eyes grew large when she heard the voice. Parker threw her hand up to stop the door from closing and pushed it back open causing the door to bump Ivy.

"What the entire hell..."

Ivy didn't finish her thought before Parker bombarded into the condo. Her eyes got even bigger seeing Assent wrapped in only a sheet, standing in the middle of the entryway. Parker paused for a moment before she allowed her emotions to completely take over.

"I can't believe you would do this to me... you fuckin' bitch!"

Assent had no opportunity to respond as Parker came charging in her direction. Assent threw her arms up to protect herself and the silken sheet fell to the floor. Parker grabbed Assent and the two became entangled.

"The fuck is your problem, Parker?"

"You cunt bitch!"

The words flew as did their bodies. One of them slipped on the silk sheet and they both ended up toppling to the floor. Ivy stood back and watched. Assent was holding her own against Parker and that pissed Parker off even more. Wild swings, hair pulling, fists flying...

It became rather comical to Ivy and she found herself giggling at first and then full on laughing at the two women, one completely naked, tussling on her ebony hardwood floor. Ivy's laughter is what stopped the brouhaha.

"What the hell is so funny, Ivy," Parker asked. The two were still tangled up. Parker was winded from the scuffle and her pale skin was bright red from the struggle. Assent managed to push Parker off and stood to her feet. She didn't look any worse for the wear.

"Psychotic, bitch," Assent spat as she smoothed her hair and put her hands on her hips. Ivy looked at Assent, a silent check in. Assent nodded. She was good. Looking back at Parker, lying in a pile on the floor, completely disheveled, Ivy started laughing again. Assent joined in. The whole thing was actually kind of funny.

Their cackles infuriated the bruised Parker.

"What the fuck is so funny?" Parker yelled and then started to tear up. The nasally whiny cry irritated Ivy.

"Stop being such a fuckin' white girl and get yo ass up off my damn floor…"

Assent stifled a giggle as she moved and stood slightly behind Ivy, casually laying her arm around Ivy's tight waist.

Seeing the two of them standing together made Parker feel even more left out.

"Why'd you do it to me, Ivy?"

Ivy looked Parker up and down but didn't respond.

"She was a gift, my way back in… you weren't supposed to keep her and not keep me!" As the color faded from Parker's skin, the red in her eyes intensified as she continued to cry.

"I'm standing right here, Parker," Assent replied offended that she was being spoken of so objectively.

Ivy turned her head slightly and pursed her lips. Assent met them with a light kiss. Parker sobbed even more.

Ivy separated herself from Assent and walked over to Parker. She wasn't laughing anymore.

"You come to my house, my house with this bullshit? Clearly, you learned nothing. There are rules to this shit, Parker... The first rule is, I decide who comes here, to my motherfuckin' house. Rule number two, if you give me a 'gift' then I decide what the fuck I want to do with it..." Ivy turned her body to the side and looked at the front door. Everyone in the room knew what that meant.

Parker dropped her head. The scolding didn't feel good and she was embarrassed; ashamed of how she acted.

With a lowered gaze, she took a tiny step toward Ivy. The crying had stopped, but now Parker was struggling to catch her breath, like a child who just got a spanking.

"Ivy... please..."

"Ivy, please what, Parker?"

"... don't send me away... I'm sorry, I'm so sorry..."

Ivy sighed deeply, having tired of the dramatics. She looked back at Parker.

"I don't do pale pussy no more... get the fuck out..."

Ivy extended her arm and Assent walked into it. The two headed back toward the bedroom leaving Parker standing alone. She watched them until the bedroom door closed, shutting her out for good.

That was Ivy's final instruction. Once again, she didn't yell; as a matter of fact, her voice was woefully calm. But the bite in her words left Parker with nothing more to say. With a final glance to the bedroom door, Parker made her exit.

After her mother's funeral, Ivy and her dad continued to live with Odessa and the boys. The next few years passed relatively quickly for Ivy. They were rather uneventful, with the exception of when her father decided he needed to spend time with his other son at Cheryl's house. Sometimes Ivy went with him; relocating with a small suitcase. Other times, her father thought it best she stay with Odessa, you know, to keep continuity with school and things. Ivy never really complained. She understood her dad and his wandering ways. Just like when she was younger, when he returned from being away, he always managed to spend extra special time with her. It might not have been going for ice cream, but he always came through.

Ivy became guardedly close to Odessa. She was not a replacement for her mother, Ivy never intended that as she wasn't close to her mother, but Odessa became like a big sister slash mother figure to her; giving her advice when solicited and giving Ivy space when she thought she needed it. Odessa always seemed cool with whatever Ivy's dad did; never verbally objecting or complaining when he was gone. Before walking out the door he would give her a kiss and say, "I'll be back." She never questioned his destination or when she could expect his return. She accepted Michael at his word.

But there was one time when Odessa wasn't so easy going with Michael's absence. Ivy overheard Odessa on the phone with a friend girl, running her father in.

"I don't know why I put up with the shit I do," Odessa complained.

"His ass been gone almost two weeks now," she continued. "He probably ain't even at Cheryl's house... probably got him another young, dumb bitch riding his jock," she continued.

Ivy continued to eavesdrop, somewhat surprised at what Odessa said, but not fully. She'd heard her mother make similar statements in the past, so someone bad mouthing her father was not completely new.

When Odessa hung up the phone, Ivy came from around the corner where she had been listening. Odessa looked surprised when she saw Michael's child standing there. She quickly turned away and busied herself straightening up the kitchen as Ivy came in.

"Why do you do it," Ivy asked taking a seat on the kitchen counter; her feet dangling inches above the floor.

"Do what," Odessa replied trying to sound innocent of the question.

"Stay with somebody who doesn't make you happy," Ivy replied matter of factly.

Odessa stopped, turned to Ivy and wiped her hands on her apron.

"What makes you think your dad doesn't make me happy?"

"Come on, Auntie O, you know I heard you."

Odessa knew Ivy overheard every word. She thought quickly on her feet. She never wanted any of the children to know what was really going on. That was familiar to Ivy as well; seeing a woman scramble for words to explain her father.

"There are times when your dad doesn't make me happy, shoot, sometimes I get real mad at him. But the thing about your dad is, when he does make me happy he makes me really happy."

Satisfied with her own response and deciding Ivy would be satisfied with it, Odessa turned back to the counter and ran water for the dishes.

"That doesn't make sense to me," Ivy interjected. "It sounds like you're making excuses for him, settling for whatever he gives you."

Ivy's words rang true in Odessa's ears, whether she wanted to hear them or not. With the boys, they didn't know any different. They were used to their father coming and going. Odessa wasn't completely sure what Ivy's experience with her dad was, but she knew what her experience was with Michael; second fiddle to Cheryl who was second fiddle to Geneva.

"That's what I'm asking, but if you don't want to answer, I get it…"

"I thought I did…"

"Not really," Ivy clarified, "Why do you settle?"

Odessa contemplated what she would say before answering Ivy. It was a hard question; one Odessa preferred not to deal with.

"I love him…"

Odessa's reply was simple and honest, but Ivy wouldn't let it go. She'd seen her mother respond the same way with her dad and she really wanted to understand why.

"So, you know he sleeps with other women, has kids by other women, barely spends time with you, but because you love him, you let him do it?"

"Chile, your dad is a grown man. One day you'll understand. You can't make a grown man do nothin' he don't wanna do."

Odessa was embarrassed by the clarity in which Ivy saw the situation and decided she wasn't answering any more questions. Hearing her own self make excuses for the things she allowed Michael to do never settled well with her, but like she said, what could she do about it?

"Tell you what, Ivy. When your dad gets back, *if he comes back*, ask him why he does what he does. He's the only one who can answer that."

Ivy accepted Odessa's resigned position. She could see her questions made Odessa uncomfortable, but speaking to her dad wouldn't explain why the women in his life were so weak. Odessa was just like her mother and Ivy soon lost patience for her. The relationship that was building between the two stifled that day.

Ivy never spoke to Odessa again about the matter. She continued to watch her dad and the women in his life. Ivy learned about love and relationships at the feet of her father.

Chapter Seven

...change is good...

Just as Ivy changed lovers, she changed locations. She grew tired of the condominium she lived in for three years. Especially after the incident with Parker; the buzzer for the door, the lack of absolute privacy. So, without much fanfare, Ivy bought a new place, something different. She moved from the center of the city to the edge of city living. It wasn't quite suburbia, but a nice blend between all things good about both locations. It was still easy access into downtown when it was necessary for her to meet with a client, but it was distant enough to where she didn't have to be bothered with neighbors if she didn't want.

True to her nature, Ivy didn't provide a forwarding address. Parker would never know her new location. Brock would know when she wanted him to. Assent... she knew from the beginning. Assent was allowed to return to Ivy's on a number of occasions. Unlike other encounters Ivy had, all her encounters with Assent were not sexual. She actually found herself enjoying having Assent around. That was new for Ivy. It wasn't just about function – someone else's ability to function at her demand, it was more than that.

Assent brought a certain kind of calm, soulful aura into Ivy's space. It was grounding. That kind of centered presence before would have certainly been a red flag for Ivy and a reason to drive that person as far away as possible. But this time, at least with Assent, it was different.

"I feel you staring at me," Ivy said sitting at her computer organizing her work on a project for a client.

Assent didn't respond, nor did she drop her gaze. Assent appreciated Ivy in all of her beauty. She was not ashamed for simply admiring her. A few more minutes passed and Assent's unwavering gaze impacted Ivy's ability to focus.

"Stop it," she demanded with a light tone, almost playful.

"I can't," Assent replied.

Reluctantly, Ivy looked up from her computer and their eyes met.

"What," Ivy inquired.

Assent remained in the spot she sat in and contemplated how she would respond. Assent was no fool. She knew Ivy's reputation and she saw how callous Ivy could be. She didn't want that for herself because she enjoyed spending time with Ivy. But Assent was not one to mince words and decided she was willing to take the risk of losing out on what had been a good thing.

"I want to know you..."

Ivy resisted her natural predilection to strike at the vulnerability Assent displayed.

"You know enough..."

Ivy adjusted her full breasts indicating the king of knowing she referred to. Assent laughed and Ivy smiled slightly. The glint in Ivy's eyes was enthralling.

Feeling as though she satisfactorily addressed the matter, Ivy went back to what she was doing and so did Assent. She continued to drink Ivy in with her eyes. After a few exaggerated moments, Ivy stopped and pushed back from her computer.

"Assent, really?"

Their eyes met again. Assent maintained her gaze without wavering. It was like a test of wills.

Assent pressed her luck.

"I want to know you…" she repeated.

This time, Assent got up from the couch and crossed the distance to where Ivy sat at her desk. Dropping to her knees so she could look Ivy directly in her eyes, Assent placed her hands on Ivy's cocoa brown thighs.

"Oh, if that's what you wanted, all you had to do was say so," Ivy said pulling up the hem of her silk slip to expose her nakedness underneath. Ivy started to reposition herself in the chair to give Assent the best possible angle to please her. Assent halted her movement and attempted to refocus Ivy's attention. She reached for Ivy's face, gently placing her hands on her cheeks and looked deeply into Ivy's eyes.

"I want to know you…"

She saw it. There was sincerity there. Ivy smiled, not because she was flattered by Assent's words and her articulated desires, but by how ballsy she was. But Ivy was not one to show weakness.

"You know enough."

Ivy's phone rang. Ivy got up from her desk and left the room. Assent knew what dismissal looked like. Ordinarily, this would be the time when she would gather her things and leave Ivy's home. But she didn't. Assent decided to wait Ivy out. She desired to know the real Ivy. Assent wasn't going to be satisfied until she did. It was a risk she was willing to take.

When Ivy reentered the room, she was fully dressed. She was rushing and didn't seem quite herself.

"Babe, something the matter?"

"Where the fuck are my keys," Ivy said flipping boxes as she looked around. Assent got up and walked over to where Ivy was searching.

"Ivy, wassup," Assent asked concerned.

"It's my dad..."

Ivy dropped her purse and her shoulders slumped. Assent saw sadness and worry in her eyes.

"Give me a sec, I'll come with..."

Ivy didn't object. She was actually relieved she wouldn't have to do this by herself. Within minutes, Assent was dressed. She found the keys Ivy had been searching for.

"I got you... I'll drive..."

Normally calm, cool and collected, Ivy was everything but that as she made her way to the hospital room where her father was. Cheryl was rather evasive on the telephone, but when Ivy walked into the room and saw her father, her heart broke a little and her knees buckled. Assent was behind Ivy to steady her as she made her way into the room. Ivy approached the bed slowly and stood over her father. His eyes were closed. Ivy turned to Assent and the look on her face asked the question her lips dared not form.

Assent nodded her head and looked at the machine attached to Ivy's dead; directing Ivy with her eyes to look there as well. Ivy followed Assent's lead and finally registered in her mind and her heart what the machine recorded. He was still alive. The beeps from the machine said so. Breathing a fraction easier, Ivy slowly reached her hand out to touch her dad's arm. She needed to touch him to confirm his body was still warm.

When she touched him and found his flesh reflective of someone who was still on this side of the living, Ivy sighed deeply. Her father started to stir. It took him a moment to open his eyes, but when he did, they quickly fixed on his daughter. Their eyes met and Michael smiled. Ivy began to tear up, relieved that her dad was still with her.

"No crying, baby girl," Michael said. His voice was gruff and raspy but his speech was clear.

Obedient to her father's instruction, Ivy quickly wiped the brimming tears from her eyes.

Assent took a few steps back to allow the two uninterrupted time together. But then the door swung open and Cheryl came in. She looked Assent up and down before crossing the room and plopping down on the bed next to Ivy's dad.

"I see you made it," Cheryl said grabbing Michael's hand and stroking it as she spoke.

Ivy did her best to pull it together before saying anything.

"How long have you been here," Ivy asked.

"Not long," her dad replied. His breathing was labored. Ivy could tell it was taking him some effort to speak.

"How long is not long?" Ivy felt her internal temperature rise, but she squelched it as best she could.

"…not long…" her dad replied.

"Why didn't you call me when it first happened?"

Ivy asked the question of her father, but it was pointed at Cheryl. Cheryl felt Ivy's razor sharp glare but didn't look up. She continued to stroke Michaels hand like it was a much-loved pet.

"I didn't want you to worry."

"Worry me? C'mon dad, you know better than that…"

Her dad's gaze dropped as he looked away.

"He didn't want to worry you, Ivy," Cheryl chimed in uninvited. "Now, stop badgering your father. He needs his rest." There was a taste of condescension in Cheryl's voice and Ivy had no tolerance for it.

Assent saw Ivy's hands close into fists and she stepped up behind Ivy and put her hand on Ivy's shoulder.

Michael looked up at his daughter. He knew her all too well. His eyes begged for Ivy to let it go, but she couldn't.

"Regardless of what my father may have wanted, why didn't you call me when it happened?"

"I wouldn't go against your father's wishes, Ivy," Cheryl stated, continuing to stroke his hand. "You're here now, that's all that matters, right, daddy?"

"That's not all that matters. The minute you found out he was sick, you should have called me. The minute he got to the hospital, you should have called me... damn what he said, I'm his daughter!"

"Now, what I'm not going to do is be chastised by a child," Cheryl quipped.

"I'm his child, his, and don't you ever forget it!"

"Don't fight..." Michael weakly interjected.

"Then you betta regulate your side piece to her place," Ivy snapped.

"Come on, Ivy," Assent said.

"Michael, now, I'm not gone stand for that," Cheryl exclaimed getting up from the bed and grabbing her purse. "I'll be back once she's gone."

"I ain't leaving," Ivy said over her shoulder as Cheryl stormed out.

"Hmph..." Cheryl grunted as she swung the door wide.

The door closed behind her and Ivy went around the bed and sat next to her father.

"Ivy," her father began.

"I know, dad, but that was foul and you know it. Forget about her, what are the doctor's saying?"

Michael looked over at Assent who was standing in the background. He smiled and she smiled in return.

"Well, at least introduce me to your friend before I put all my personal business out there."

"Dad, Assent; Assent, this is my dad."

"It's nice to meet you, Mr. Sims," Assent replied stepping closer to the bed.

"Pretty and polite," Michael replied.

"Back off, old man," Ivy quipped.

He laughed and the two laughed with him. It was a good way to lighten the mood in the room.

"So…" Ivy redirected the conversation, but her father tried to keep it light.

"They said it was a heart attack," Michael replied.

"Oh, dad. I'm so sorry," Ivy said reaching over and touching her father on the arm. "So, what's next? How long do you have to stay, what are the doctor's recommending?"

"Slow down baby girl." Michael interrupted. "Your old man's going to be just fine," Michael said trying to reassure his only daughter.

"But I have to say, I've never felt a pain like that since the pain of losing your mom…"

Ivy was stunned by her father's comment. Dad didn't cry at the funeral and he never really talked about her mother much after she was gone. Ivy always thought her mom was just one of many, but what her father said cast a different light. She looked at her father and saw the sincerity in his eyes.

As if answering the question Ivy didn't ask, Michael spoke.

"I know my actions probably didn't show it, but I loved Geneva. The first woman I ever truly loved… I miss her…"

Maybe the health scare was making her dad soft. Ivy wasn't sure, but this was certainly an eye-opening conversation. It gave Ivy much to think about long after the conversation was over.

Michael was quiet for a moment and then his tone became very serious.

"Don't be afraid to love, Ivy, you hear me? Don't be afraid to open your heart and let somebody in."

"You dying or something, old man?" Ivy said trying to light the heavy intonations.

"No, you will be stuck with me for a while, but I mean it, Ivy. I didn't set a good example for you, but it doesn't mean I don't want the best for you. Just be open to the possibilities, okay?"

Ivy and Assent stayed with her father long into the night. She visited him in the hospital every day until he was released. Even though they had always been in touch, Ivy made sure to speak with her father every day to make sure he was doing okay. She never forgot what he said, no matter how hard she tried.

Chapter Eight

... quiet time ...

Ivy settled into her new home only after things with her father settled down. She found herself restless and desirous of something she hadn't had in a while. The text message went out. New address and a time. That was it. She knew he would respond.

When the doorbell rang, Ivy allowed herself a smile. He was punctual as expected. He knew she despised tardiness and that was enough to get you dismissed. Ivy opened the door to see Brock standing there with a sultry smile on his face from ear to ear.

"Nice place... I missed you..."

He followed Ivy in, taking in the new sights as they moved through the massive home. Out of the corner of his eye, Brock saw a beautiful, black woman sitting on the couch reading a book. Even seated, he could appreciate how attractive she was. Assent looked up from her book long enough to flash a smile in Brock's direction.

"Hi there," Brock said trying too hard to sound sexy.

"Hi," Assent replied snickering at his overzealous attempt.

Ivy never broke her stride. There would be time to introduce the two but tonight was not it. Brock quickly fell back in step. The sultry sway of Ivy's hips quickly reeled him back in. Assent returned to her book. The slight smile on her face was still there.

Ivy entered the expansive master bedroom. Brock appreciated the luxury of the space only momentarily as he made a bee line for Ivy. She had kept him at bay longer than usual and he craved spending quality time with her. Brock never sought solace in the company of another woman when he was on forced hiatus from Ivy. She was too much to measure up to and he'd rather not bother with second rate.

Before he could plant his lips to hers, Ivy put her hand up.

"Shower…"

Brock scoffed and shrugged his shoulders. If that would please Ivy, he had no problem with it.

The master bath was attached to her bedroom so Brock made his way inside. The luxury continued, in cool greys and stainless steel. Brock turned on the multiple shower heads in the walk-in shower and quickly disrobed. The faster he got this part handled, the faster he could get to his Ivy. The aurora marble floor tiles were cool to his feet, but once Brock stepped inside the shower, he warmed up quickly. He let the streams of warm water flow over his head and reached for the soap to lather up.

Just then the bathroom door opened and Ivy stepped inside. The sheer taupe sheath she wore looked magnificent against her cocoa skin. It fit in all the right places, accentuating her curves and fell away ethereally; giving the illusion of floating. Brock looked up as she allowed the sheath to cascade to the floor, revealing her hot body. Brock's body reacted; his manhood going from flaccid to full on in a matter of seconds. How he missed her so… The erection happened so fast it hurt. Brock stroked himself to ease some of the pain. The warm water hitting against his member intensified his hard on and Brock moaned under the pressure.

"You're not going to wait for me," Ivy teased.

"Get your ass in here…"

Ivy allowed Brock that brief moment of being in control. She missed him… really, she missed a good fuck so enter the shower she did. There was no time for precursory fondling and kissing. There was no time for mood setting or gushing emotions. Beneath the cascade of water, Brock turned Ivy around so her back was to him. She bent slightly at the waist and he bent at the knee, giving him just the right angle to enter her smooth pussy from behind.

Ivy's pussy was nice and tight, not having been penetrated by a cock in a while. Brock appreciated the friction against his rock-hard dick. His desire to plunge himself inside her was momentarily halted by the tightness of her walls. It wasn't an unpleasant problem to have. He had to slow down and take a few short strokes before maximum penetration.

Ivy's ass sat perfectly atop him and Brock had to restrain himself from cumming too soon. When he finally broke through to the Promised Land, his body quivered and her back arched. Brock didn't even try to restrain himself. He craved Ivy like a junkie craved a fix and he let her know.

"Shit I missed this…"

"Shut up and fuck me…"

That was the command, the control he liked. Brock did as he was told and got down to the business of rocking Ivy's jewel. Putting one hand against the shower wall, Ivy braced herself against the thrusts. With the other she reached underneath and cradled his ball sack, sending Brock into overdrive. He was almost frantic as his cock moved against her inner walls. Ivy rode his wave and pushed against him for deep penetration. He hit her pearl over and over. Ivy was on the verge of her own explosion. Brock wrapped his arms around her and cupped her taut breasts. The pressure against her hardened nipples sent a new sensation to Ivy's box and hot warmth released between her thighs. Her gism coated Brock's cock and he felt her puss contract, release, and contract again. He couldn't hold it and he didn't try.

"… uh… uh… uhh… uhhh… uhhhhh…"

Brock shot his load deep inside Ivy's cavernous walls but she didn't let him go. She tightened her walls around his near flaccid cock and held it captive; prisoner to her pussy's whims… Ivy wanted every drop of what Brock had to give and so she milked his dick, flexing and releasing; allowing it to slide to the point of escape and then masterfully reeling it back in. Brock damn near lost his mind; his body quaking under her skilled touch. He held her tightly, never wanting to let go and nibbled her neck, kissing her ear and allowing her to strip him of the last hot drop.

When she was done, Ivy allowed Brock's member to be released. She turned in his arms and the two stood face to face. She kissed him deeply and a new wave of electricity shot through Brock's willing body. Freeing her arms, Ivy placed a hand on Brock's head and pushed. She didn't have to indicate any further what needed to happen next. Brock dropped down to his knees as the warmth of the shower continued to beat against his muscular body. Lifting one of Ivy's legs over his shoulder, she leaned into the corner of the shower as Brock's lips found her lips. He opened them with his tongue and licked her inner puss. He tasted the comingling inside her and plunged his tongue deep. Ivy's head fell back between her shoulders as she pressed against his pert tongue. She still had more to give. Brock brought a new wave of orgasm to Ivy and she fucked his face, covering his mouth with newfound wetness.

Knowing she was satisfied, at least for the moment, Brock stood up and allowed the water to wash over him again. Ivy stepped out of the shower, grabbed a towel and began to dry off. Brock followed suit, hoping she wasn't done with him. He wanted to be with her even more. This was not the time for a quick dismissal. Before exiting the bathroom, Ivy touched a button on the wall and a line of communication came to life.

"Assent, I need you upstairs..."

Brock smiled. Maybe he would get a chance to meet the beautiful woman downstairs after all.

Assent made her way into the master bedroom. Ivy's body still glistened with moisture from the shower. Assent felt a tingling in her own hot box. Assent made her way over to Ivy and the two kissed, long and deep.

"Brock, this is Assent. She was a gift..."

Brock's member started to rise again. Girl on girl always got him going.

"Nice to meet you, Assent."

Assent smiled and looked at Ivy for permission. Ivy nodded slightly and Assent walked the short distance to Brock and kissed him full on. Brock's naked body tensed and his battery instantly recharged. Ivy walked up behind Assent and reached around her stroking Brock's head. The three interchanged sweet and deep kisses as the temperature between the trio rose. Brock looked to Ivy before he made a move. She was the conductor of this ménage and he didn't dare move prematurely. With her non-verbal permission, Brock began to unbutton Assent's shirt, releasing her tight breasts from the oversized shirt she wore. His dick got hard. Ivy lifted Assent's shirt from her shoulders and allowed it to fall to the carpeted floor. The only thing that remained to be removed was a delicate pair of lace panties that barely covered Assent's muff.

"Leave it," Ivy said as she turned and walked towards the bed. Ivy sat down of the edge of the large bed and Assent sat down next to her. Brock made his way over not sure what Ivy wanted the next move to be. No matter what it was, Brock was sure he would enjoy it.

Ivy took Brock's cock into her hand and kissed the tip. She then offered it to Assent who kissed the tip as well. Ivy was not averse to sharing. She always intended to share Brock with Assent, but she needed to have him first; to get the first of what he had to give. And now that that was done, the three could play. Ivy kissed Brock's tip again and then opened her mouth to receive more of him into her warm mouth. The muscles in Brock's legs tensed as he looked down at Ivy suckling his member. Assent joined in, licking further down Brock's cock and tickling his balls with her tongue. Ivy placed her hand on Assent's thigh and Assent guided Ivy's hand underneath her panties to her own sweet spot. Ivy slowly rubbed Assent's outer walls before inserting one then two fingers into her welcoming wetness.

Brock reached down and found Assent's breasts. He rolled her nipples between his fingers as the intensity between the three grew. Ivy released Brock from her lips and leaned over and kissed Assent full on the mouth. She moved Assent underneath her and Assent laid back on the bed. With Ivy on top, Brock slid his hard cock into Ivy's upturned pussy as she continued to kiss Assent. Ivy found Assent's breasts and sucked on them, one and then the other as Brock found a nice slow stroke that titillated her jewel. Assent wrapped her legs around Ivy's waist and with the slightest adjustment, Brock moved from Ivy's goodness to the newness of the one who lay beneath. She reached down and moved her panties to the side, allowing Brock inside her.

"Oh shit..." Brock said breathlessly as he slid in and out of Assent. She appreciated his manly touch and pulled Ivy up to her mouth, deep throating her with a long kiss.

"This is nice," Assent said smiling at Ivy. The two snickered as Brock found his way back to Ivy's warmth. Brock continued to slow stroke Assent, feeling her walls give underneath his member. Assent allowed her feet to return to the bed as Brock hit the top of her wall. Ivy lifted herself and moved further up the bed, watching as Brock found a nice rhythm with Assent.

This is nice, Ivy thought to herself as Assent's back arched and her body convulsed. His thighs slapped against Assent's ass in syncopated rhythm. Assent moaned and Ivy smiled. Brock was on the brink of his own explosion, but he didn't want Assent to have it. That was reserved for Ivy. Riding Assent's climax, he steeled himself so as not to blow. Brock released her and gently removed himself from within her. Brock walked around the side of the bed and reached for Ivy, as he sat down. She climbed on top, one foot on each side of him and lowered herself onto his coated cock. Ivy took Brock all the way in to the hilt and then lowered herself, sitting on his strong thighs. She didn't move. He didn't move.

Brock's cock throbbed inside Ivy' swollen walls. He didn't move. She didn't move. Ivy looked into Brock's eyes. There was a wildness just beyond the warmth, right past the familiar. Brock wrapped his arms around Ivy's waist as she started to gently rock back and forth. His cock was pressed against her pearl. Her walls enveloped him. The gentle tilt from the rocking continued to press against every facet of Ivy's clit. Brock's body quivered. It took everything in him not to explode. Ivy continued to rock, stretching and elongating her upper body while her puss held Brock tight.

The pressure mounted. Just when Brock didn't think he could hold on any longer, Ivy leaned back away from him, deeply arching her back, shortening her vaginal canal.

"Ah shit, girl," Brock whispered. His thigh muscles tightened again as he resisted the urge to thrust. The veins in his hardened member strained as Ivy repositioned herself, placing her hands on his shoulders and lifting off to the point that only the tip remained inside her. Brock felt cool air at the base of his cock. And then Ivy descended on him, taking him fully back inside herself.

"Keep still," Ivy directed as she started to stroke him, up and down, slow lift to slow descent. As her rise and fall sped up Brock grabbed Ivy's plump ass and squeezed. Ivy shortened her stroke and started to pump faster. Brock lifted himself to meet her and Ivy smiled. She had given him permission and Brock took it. He growled as he pushed up meeting her push down.

"Cum with me," Ivy said.

The intensity and the speed of the fuck increased to a near frantic pace. Brock held on tight as Ivy sat flush against him, letting him fuck her. He fucked hard as Ivy wrapped her arms around his neck.

"...mmmm..." Ivy moaned as hot gism spilled from her puss. Brock's member shook and then released, splaying Ivy's inner walls fully with his cum. After a few moments, Brock turned on the bed and laid Ivy down. Assent met her at the top of the bed and Brock found himself a place to nestle in behind. They stayed that way until morning's light found them.

Chapter Nine

...togetherness...

Brock was allowed to stay around for the next few days. The three ate together, watched movies together, laughed together, enjoyed each other and fucked together. It was reminiscent of older times for Brock and Ivy. There was something comforting about the familiar for Ivy and she liked it. At the same time, Ivy didn't allow that feeling to remain. She didn't want to get comfortable in it. Comforting yes. Comfortable, no. Comfortable for Ivy meant complacent. Complacency allowed people to take advantage of the notion that you would always be there, like a door mat that they could walk over because they were allowed to get comfortable. Ivy saw what comfortable did to her mother. She saw what comfortable did to Odessa and even Cheryl. Ivy saw how their ability to get comfortable with her father's absence and presence diminished them. She would never allow herself to be diminished.

And just as Brock had been invited in, he was dismissed. Brock was used to it and didn't voice any objection when Ivy told him she would see him later. That later could mean tomorrow, a week, a month from now. That was okay. He would be there when she welcomed him back in.

When it was just the two of them again, Assent pursued a line of conversation she started before.

"As much time as we've spent together, Ivy, I feel like there's so much more I don't know about you."

Ivy smacked her lips and took a sip of the Merlot she was enjoying.

"You know enough," she replied sitting the glass down on the coffee table in front of her.

"Okay," Assent replied. "Is there anything you want to know about me," she asked, changing directions.

"I know enough," Ivy said.

Assent was taken aback by her response. She shouldn't have been, but she was. Teetering on the edge of making a fatal mistake, Assent pressed the matter.

"So you're content with not letting me get to know you better, you only knowing what you know of me?"

"Yes."

Ivy's response was flat yet definitive.

Assent was saddened by her aloofness. She wanted to connect with Ivy in a deeper way, much more than physical. She enjoyed what she knew of Ivy, but there was so much more lurking behind the shadows and Assent wanted a glimpse; insight into the woman behind the distant exterior.

"I can't do this anymore..."

"Do what," Ivy asked intrigued yet miffed by Assent's response. Ivy knew she pushed people away, but they fought to stay. She didn't expect that Assent would allow herself to be pushed out.

"Be only to you what you let me. There's more to me than that. Hell, there's more to you than that. If you won't let me in, I'm not going to fight to get there."

Ivy picked up her glass and took another sip. She watched as Assent got up from the couch and disappeared up the stairs. When Assent returned a few minutes later with a bag on her shoulder, Ivy didn't respond. She could try to stop her, try to convince Assent to stay, that she wanted her to stay, but she didn't.

In silence, Assent put her shoes on, grabbed her purse and her keys and made her exit. For the first time in a long time, Ivy was all alone; alone with her own thoughts; alone with her own feelings.

Ivy invited her dad over for a little father daughter time. He hadn't seen her new place and she wanted to share it with the most important person in her life. Michael was impressed with his daughter's new home and told her how proud he was of her. Ivy and her father sat down to a meal she prepared and they laughed and talked over a good meal. After dinner, the two retired to Ivy's library. The lighting in the room was low and the floor to ceiling shelves were covered with books from classics to women's fiction. The two sat down in the oversized matching leather arm chairs that sat in the middle of the room.

Ivy poured bourbon for the two of them as they settled in.

"How you feeling, dad? The truth," Ivy encouraged.

"I have my good days and bad days, but overall, I'm good."

"I worry about you, if you're taking care of yourself, doing what you're supposed to do?"

"I know you do, but you shouldn't. I'm good, for real. Your dad is always going to be good. Besides, Odessa and Cheryl make sure I'm following the doctors' orders."

Ivy smiled.

"Don't mention that witch's name in my house."

"Stop it," Michael laughingly chastised.

"I'm so serious," Ivy replied. "I dunno why you keep her around anyway."

"Who, Odessa?"

"No, that troll, Cheryl…"

"Ivy Frances Renee, you know better than that," Michael chided.

"But seriously, dad, she is not a nice woman. I mean she seemed nice when I was a kid, but she's too possessive, she's forgotten her place."

He recognized what was going on with his daughter.

"Ivy, you will always have first place in my heart, know that."

"I do, I know…"

"But?"

Ivy hesitated, having never traversed down this line of conversation with her father before.

"As much as mom loved you, doted on you, you still found the need for these other people, these other women."

Now it was Michael's turn to be quiet. He always moved through his life as if the things he did didn't bother him no matter how his actions impacted others. What Ivy didn't know was that at times, his choices did bother him. He felt responsible for a lot of pain in the lives of a lot of people. He just never gave voice to it.

"That was my own insecurity. It had nothing to do with your mother. It wasn't her fault I wandered."

"But you were so brazen with it. You didn't try to hide it and they didn't make you. They just let you do whatever the hell you wanted to do with no consequence."

"There were consequences, Ivy. Don't ever think there weren't. I paid for my decisions in ways you may never understand. But you will if you don't change."

"How did this conversation get to be about me?"

"Because I see so much of me in you."

"I am my father's daughter," Ivy quipped.

"Yes, you are, but I want more for you than that," Michael replied.

"It worked for you all these years. Odessa and Cheryl are still holding on," Ivy reminded.

"Yeah, from the outside it looks like it worked. I ain't gone lie, having choices has its benefits. When one of them got on my nerves, yeah, I had another place to lay my head until they got on my nerves too. But that really ain't no way to live."

"What do you mean, dad?"

"It was like I was always on the move, running from what made me uncomfortable. I don't like conflict, never have, so as soon as I felt tension in a situation, I moved to the next. The problem with that is, you never get resolution. The conflict festers and you never work through it to get things back to what initially brought you and that person together in the first place."

Michael fell quiet and took a long sip of his bourbon.

"That's what happened with me and your mom. She saw some things in me she didn't like, didn't appreciate... the disrespect. When she called me on it, of course I didn't want to hear it, so I physically moved to the next. But my heart stayed where I left. I didn't like hurting your mother but more than that, I hated seeing the disappointment in her eyes because of the choices I made. My choices made your mother sad."

Ivy listened intently as her dad poured out his heart. This was a side of her father she'd only had a glimpse of in the past.

"Your mother wasn't weak, Ivy. I know that's what you thought, that's what you think, but she wasn't a weak woman. Your mother was the strongest woman I know. And you need to recognize that."

"She was strong because she put up with me. She could have easily kept me from you, hell, divorced me... kept the madness from her front door, but she didn't. Your mother put you before herself. She put me before her own feelings and she kept our little family together. I was the one who didn't appreciate just how much she loved me. And she loved me hard. Geneva was the best thing that ever happened to me... she loved me even with all my faults and flaws... she gave me you..."

The two were quiet and both were contemplative.

"You are more like me than any of the boys," Michael continued breaking the silence between father and daughter.

"Does that really surprise you, dad?"

"Not at all," Michael laughed.

"But your brothers are starting to settle down, even Rod, and you know how wild he was."

"Now that does surprise me," Ivy replied.

"I want that for you too, Ivy. It's time for you to settle down."

"Why, you still haven't."

"But that's where you're wrong," Michael corrected.

"It may not have been with one person, but I've been settled for years. There hasn't been anyone new in my life. I never introduced you or your brothers to anybody new. Think about it. I have been with the same women for a long time. That's settled."

"I'm not saying run off and get married. I know that's not your nature. But just like I told you before, you have to be willing to let someone in, let them get to know all the best parts of you that I know you hide away. You are my child, I know that about you. Settle down in your own way, but settle down before the one's that really love you get away."

Ivy had no quirky comeback behind what her dad said. But his words forced her to look at his situation differently. What he said was true. Odessa and that wretch Cheryl had been around since she was a little girl. They were consistent. The relationships stayed the same. Although they may have been tested, his relationships never wavered.

Long after her father left for the evening, Ivy thought about what he said, especially about her mom. Could she have been wrong about her mother all this time? Ivy thought her father cheated on her because she was weak, but he didn't see her that way. He saw her mother as strong; the strongest woman he ever knew. That's how he described her. Maybe Ivy took the wrong cue and saw things from her own slighted vantage point; not being able to appreciate her mother for the strength she did show. Her mother, in her own way, shielded Ivy from her father's wandering ways for as long as she could and even when his cheating breached their door, Geneva continued to protect Ivy. She kept their home life stable and balanced for as long as she could.

Thinking about her mother made Ivy sad. For the entirety of her life, Ivy underestimated her mother and treated her badly because of it. She saw her mother as a poor example of a woman, allowing a man to take advantage of her. But maybe that wasn't really what it was. Maybe Ivy couldn't see her mother as strong because to see her that way would force Ivy to see her dad as the one with the flaws. His philandering would then be put into full view and she would have to reckon with the fact that any instability she experienced in her young life was because of his selfish ways. The dad she idolized, that she held in such high regard, would have been diminished by his own insecurities and frailties. Ivy would have been forced to consider that her father was the one in the wrong, all this time... all her life... even now...

Her mother was gone and now Ivy couldn't go back and fix it. Ivy allowed herself to sit with that unpleasant emotion as much as it pained her. She resisted the urge to deny how bad it felt, to run away from the rawness of her feelings. Ivy sat with it and allowed herself to really feel the feelings of sadness and grief. She hadn't really grieved the loss of her mother; instead relegating her absence to one of life's casualties. But to hear her father speak, Geneva's

121

suicide was a casualty of the war her dad waged on Geneva's heart.

The realness of Ivy's uncapped emotions caused her to consider something more of what her father said, that she shouldn't be like him; that she should allow herself to love and be loved before it was too late. There were people in Ivy's life who loved her. She knew that to be true. Their undying devotion was more than just physical attraction and they tried to tell her, to show her that they truly cared for her. But Ivy shut them out and shut off her feelings. Ivy thought it selfish even self-serving and she had always been okay with that. Ivy never considered the reason she didn't allow anyone in was because she didn't want to be vulnerable to the pain love could cause. Maybe...

Chapter Ten

... just Ivy...

Ivy was alone by choice. Her aloneness lasted for a few months. At times, she was tempted to call on a lover or two to fill the void, but she resisted the temptation. She resisted the urge for temporary pleasure. Instead, Ivy dove head first into her work, filling her days with meetings and consultations or spending her evenings tucked away in her library reconnecting with her love of reading. Ivy spent a lot of her quiet time with her own unfiltered thoughts. She accomplished a lot in her young life, despite the hardships and tragedies she experienced early on.

That was something Ivy could be proud of and she was. But her father's words of caution continued to haunt her despite her strong will. Ivy was listening.

As she lay in her massive bed, it all of a sudden felt too big for just her. She missed them... him... Ivy missed her. Assent left an indelible impression on Ivy's near hardened heart. And she did it without effort. That's what troubled Ivy the most about Assent. She didn't do anything special, she didn't work extra hard to impress Ivy. Assent was just Assent. That was it. Ivy didn't have to work extra hard with Assent. She was drama free; a quiet, confident calm that offered balance to Ivy. And if Ivy allowed herself to think about it, Assent felt like enough of a woman for her. But Ivy had to be honest with herself. One woman would never be enough. She need the juxtaposition of masculinity that only a man could provide. That man had always been Brock. He didn't require a lot either, but for different reasons. Brock was easy because Ivy taught him to be easy; not because that was his natural predilection. Brock understood Ivy's wayward ways and her shielded heart and he accepted it. There were moments, early on, when Brock tried to be possessive; be the only lover in Ivy's life but she taught him very quickly how she operated. Either he got with the program or she would cut him out. Brock never wanted that. He always wanted to be a part of Ivy's inner circle; no matter how big or small his part would be. Yes, that's what was easy about Brock. He understood his place.

Ivy would invite him back in. That was an easy decision. Ivy wanted easy right now. Assent she craved, but Ivy knew Assent had the ability to walk away thereby making her less than easy to deal with. Ivy understood in order for Assent to return, she would have to bear more than her perky breasts to her. Ivy would have to get emotionally naked and reveal the truth of who she is. Ivy wasn't sure she wanted to deal with that. Her emotions were still raw. Her feelings were still spilling out at the most inopportune time. Ivy wasn't ready to come soul to soul with Assent. That would be the requirement. She would have to meet the requirement of another person and Ivy didn't want to deal with it. No, she would choose Brock. He had no requirements of her. He still knew how to behave. He would assuage her loneliness and give her sentiments time to fade to the background where Ivy liked to keep them. Besides, at one point, Ivy considered Brock permanent, like "the one" she could live the rest of her life with. Maybe she wasn't wrong about that. Maybe she could 'settle' with Brock. Just maybe with Brock around, all thoughts of Assent would fade too. At least, that's what Ivy hoped.

And just as Ivy predicted, she and Brock fell into an easy pattern of existence. The conversation was simple, the sex was magnificent, the pressure was nil. Brock busied himself when Ivy needed her space and was readily available to her when she wanted him around. Brock was glad to be back too. He loved Ivy in a way that was easy for him. He didn't have to be overly romantic, play games, or work hard to entice her to his sexual desires. Ivy was demanding, but not in the ways other women were. She didn't demand time and attention and affection and flowery words of love. Ivy made no demands that his heart or his body only belong to her. She just needed him totally available to her when she needed him to be, not all the time. There was no ball and chain feeling of committed relationship with Ivy. It was always wild and unpredictable while at the same time being easy and comfortable. But when they met in that sacred space, just the two of them where their bodies and minds joined together, Brock and Ivy had made a connection that neither time nor space could diminish. Brock lived for those times, those moments, and for him, that was enough.

And everything was great, for a while. But Ivy was never one to be completely satisfied for too long and so she let Brock in on what she wanted next.

Freedom was brought into a situation that would be mutually satisfying to everyone; at least that's how it was described to him. Ivy wanted more than what she had with a single lover.

He knew Brock before. They met innocently enough at a business function. Brock was in corporate sales and Freedom was in marketing. They had mutual business interests and were drawn to each other in the beginning because of it. They had drinks together and Freedom thought something more than just business was there, but he was hesitant to let Brock know just how attracted to him he was. Who wouldn't be? Brock was fine, plain and simple. He stood 5'11" tall, lean in all the right places and thick in those that mattered most. He was pleasing to the eye and he knew it. That air of confidence was sexy as hell to Freedom. Brock was a man's man. It was only when they got to know each other better, away from business that he learned an unsuspected side of Brock.

But even then, Freedom didn't show all his cards. It was late one night. Freedom and Brock happened to be at a bar they both frequented. They shared laughs and drinks. Brock had an especially tough week and was letting off some steam. This particular night Freedom noticed Brock drank more than usual. When Brock suggested they leave the bar and find someplace quiet to chat Freedom wasn't quite sure what to expect, but he was open to whatever. It wasn't long before they were back at his place. Soft music, a lit fire and a few more drinks later, Brock came on to him. A part of Freedom wanted to dismiss it as the antics of a drunken man. The other part of Freedom, the one who wanted Brock won out.

It was one kiss, then two; the second one deeper and more intense than the first. Brock sat his glass on the table, unbuttoned the first few buttons on Freedom's shirt and looked at Freedom in such a way that gave him permission to return the gesture. When he unbuttoned Brock's shirt revealing the beginnings of his strong chiseled chest, Freedom allowed himself to let go and Brock encouraged him; pulling his shirt out of his pants and lying back on the couch. Freedom accepted the invitation. Brock opened his legs and Freedom moved between them. He unbuttoned the rest of Brock's shirt and let it fall away from his body. He kissed Brock from his neck down to his firm abs. Freedom felt Brock's cock pressing against his stomach as he retraced his steps and sucked Brock's pert nipple.

Brock moaned under Freedom's touch. For Freedom, the ambiance faded. All he saw, all he wanted was the delicious man in front of him. Unbuckling Brock's belt and unzipping his pants, Freedom allowed his hand to trace Brock's firmness. It felt good to him. Brock reached down and freed himself from the constraints of his boxer briefs. Freedom smiled at the thickness he was presented with. The slight curve of Brock's dick was just to his liking. Wanting him unrestricted, Freedom backed away enough so that Brock could remove the clothes that served to inhibit him. He stood immediately in front of Freedom who couldn't wait any longer. He kissed the tip of Brock's cock and tasted the pre-cum that formed there. Brock moaned again as Freedom pulled his ten-inch cock slowly into his mouth.

Freedom's suck was firm. His own member was now engorged. He was completely turned on by the man standing before him. Grabbing Brock by the ass, he pulled him forward pushing the chocolate dong deeper into his throat. Brock grabbed the base of his cock, stretching the skin to its tightest and plunged himself deeper. Freedom groaned and the vibration echoed through Brock's dick. He mouth fucked him harder, hitting the back of Freedom's throat repeatedly with enough force to gag him. Freedom loved it.

The thrusts intensified and Freedom rode each one not allowing Brock's cock to escape his lips. Brock was on the verge of shooting his wad, but he wanted more. He leaned down and placed his hands on Freedom's shoulders. Freedom looked up hoping that this wasn't the end of the pleasure.

"Stand up for me."

Without dropping his gaze, Freedom stood to his feet; his cock poking awkwardly through the front of his pants. Brock rubbed against it with a strong hand. Then he turned Freedom away from him. Reaching from behind, he helped Freedom unzip his pants that then fell to the floor. Brock rubbed Freedom's manhood again, squeezing it with just enough force to make Freedom moan with pleasure. Freedom reached behind and pulled Brock closer to him feeling Brock's still erect cock against his ass. Brock leaned in, pressing against him harder. Freedom pushed against him, relishing in his touch. He only broke away from full contact long enough to reach into a small silver box on the cocktail table to retrieve a condom.

"Undress."

Freedom did so willingly as Brock unwrapped the prophylactic and smoothed it on his pulsing cock. He didn't wait. As soon as the rubber was secured he bent Freedom over. Licking his index and middle fingers, Brock found Freedom's asshole and wet it, inserting one finger than the other. Freedom reached back, grabbed his cheeks and spread them wide.

"Don't tease me, Brock, fuck me." Brock was no stranger to sex with a man. There were times when he preferred it although being with a woman was most common for him. Freedom needn't say more. He guided himself in pumping slowly to break through the initial tightness.

"Yes, Brock, fuck me please!" Freedom allowed himself to get lost in the rhythm Brock moved him in. Brock placed his hands over Freedom's and pulled him back each time he thrust forward. The deep penetration made Freedom squeal with delight.

"Yes, baby, yeesss... give it to me!"

The rocking sensation intensified. Brock loved the tight squeeze of Freedom's ass canal around his hardness. Throwing his head back, he fucked him harder. The muscles in Brock's thighs tightened and released as he bent his knees then stood straight with every upward thrust. Freedom felt the curve of Brock's member pushing against the side of his opening. Easing his hands from underneath Brock's, Freedom used one hand to leverage himself against the wonderful pounding he was taking and the other to stroke his own member.

Brock rocked him harder, faster, and deeper. Freedom felt as if he would explode with the combination of the vigorous fuck he was taking the rhythm of which he mimicked with his own self stroke.

"I'm cumming motherfucka'. Fuck my ass!"

Freedom's ass tightened and throbbed around Brock's dick as he felt the convulse of Freedom shooting his gism. Brock couldn't hold any longer.

"Son of a bitch! Ugghh," Brock moaned as he unloaded thick cum into the thin layer of rubber. He allowed himself to collapse on top of Freedom's now wet back as the two of them worked up a sweat with their virgin escapade.

"Damn, man..."

Brock laughed lightly feeling fantastic. They stayed in that position until Brock's cock was flaccid. Leaning up, he grabbed the base of the rubber so it wouldn't slip and eased from the tightness that still held him. Freedom grabbed Brock by the hand and led him into the master bathroom. After turning on the shower, the condom was disposed of. Before both men stepped into the shower, Freedom knelt in front of Brock again, this time licking him clean. He felt what Brock was like, but he wouldn't be satisfied until he tasted all of what he was like. Once satisfied that he absorbed every drop of sperm Brock offered up, the two men stepped into the shower. Steam washed over their naked bodies. Before the shower was over, round two commenced. Freedom wanted to make sure Brock had nothing left to offer before he let him go.

Brock and Freedom's sexualized entanglements continued for several months, each time more intense than the last. As hard as he fought against it, Freedom started to feel something for Brock; more than lust, more than just bodily craving. This was a dangerous place for Freedom because he loved hard. In the past he may have been far too careless with his body, but never with his heart; that he protected like fine porcelain encased by even finer glass. Brock was more than just great sex. There was great conversation at a depth that stimulated Freedom's intellect. There was a suave sophistication, an effortless swagger that continued to pique his interest. Freedom couldn't forget the dimples; deep caverns that appeared with the slightest smile. On a child dimples are cute. On a grown, sexy man, they were entrancing.

There were times Freedom got the sense that his time was cut short with Brock because of someone else. Brock didn't wear a ring and when asked said he wasn't married. Although Freedom knew Brock liked being with him and maybe other men at some point, if there was someone in Brock's public life, it would be a woman. He wasn't a down low kind of dude in Freedom's estimation. Brock was private. He liked what he liked, no frills, no fuss. Freedom considered asking Brock about the other part of his life, but didn't want to risk stepping over the nonverbal boundaries he assumed were there.

One night, however, Brock brought up the conversation while the two sat in bed after an exhausting and exhilarating tryst. He told Freedom he had a lover and they were together for several years. She, Ivy, was sexy, driven, and open minded.

"She wants a threesome," he said laughingly. Freedom almost choked on the Merlot he was sipping. He sat the glass down on the night stand to avoid a spill.

"Is she serious?"

"Definitely," Brock replied. "That's just the kind of woman she is. She knows exactly what she wants." Leveling a steady, sexy gaze into Freedom's eyes, Brock continued. "And I want to give her just that."

"And you're good with it?" Freedom's curiosity was heightened.

"Hell yeah, and once you meet Ivy, you will be too."

It took Freedom a minute to realize he was being invited to the soiree.

"Oh... oh, you want me to join you and Ivy?" Freedom was flattered, intrigued and uneasy all at the same time.

Brock pulled Freedom into him so Freedom's back was to him. Freedom loved to spoon with Brock. The close proximity never failed to give him a hard on. Brock found it and stroked it to life as he continued.

"Would you do that for me?"

I'll do damn near anything for you, Freedom thought to himself, but didn't dare utter those words out loud. It would give too much away. It was too soon for Brock to really know just what kind of hold he had on Freedom.

"How can I say no when you're doing what you're doing?" Freedom collapsed back into the feeling of Brock's strong hand stroking him.

"Don't say no," Brock ratcheted up the intensity nibbling Freedom's ear and kissing him at the nape of his neck. The show of affection pushed Freedom close to the edge and he ground on Brock's stiffening member as Brock stroked him vigorously.

"Will you join us?" the warmness from his breath titillated Freedom's masculinized proclivities.

He couldn't resist cumming or Brock's suggestion.

"Yes, yes, Brock, yes…"

Chapter Eleven

… ménage a trois …

A few days later, Freedom had his first encounter with Ivy. It was overwhelming. She was overwhelming. Ivy stood 5'9, hour glass, full figure, ebony skin that looked kissed by the sun, sexy lips that hid the slightest gap between her otherwise perfect teeth. Her eyes smoldered with no effort. When Ivy looked at you, she really saw you. Freedom was smitten.

Ivy didn't waste any time. When Brock said she was no nonsense it served as an understatement. She was fiercely intense and she didn't mince words. Ivy sized Freedom up, walking slowly around him after Brock's introduction. Freedom wanted to be offended by her actions, but instead his feelings of flattery grew.

"Do you like girls, Freedom," she asked suggestively.

"Yes."

"Do you like me, Freedom?" Her voice was soft and sensual. The sexual tension in the room rose tenfold. Brock stood back with a sexy smirk on his face.

"Yes." Freedom's voice faltered slightly. She made him nervous, excited, but nervous nonetheless. Ivy continued to circle him like predator to prey.

"Do you want to fuck me, Freedom?" Ivy stopped immediately in front of him perfectly eye level. She wasn't smiling, her gaze unwavering. Freedom broke the stare and looked to Brock for permission, assurance, he wasn't sure. He wasn't able to maintain it as Ivy took a finger and repositioned Freedom's face so he could only see her.

"Do you want to fuck me, Freedom?" Her touch was like magic. It wasn't designed as an overt sexual gesture. Freedom found her redirection sexy.

"Yes, Ivy. I want to fuck all of you." Her boldness made him bold. He really did want to be inside her to see if she felt as good as she looked. Freedom was willing to see where this ménage would take him. He had nothing to lose.

Ivy crossed the living room and headed down a hallway. Brock followed after her, but stopped short when he realized Freedom was still standing where Ivy left him. Brock doubled back, grabbed Freedom by the hand and led him to the master bedroom where Ivy was there waiting.

"I want you to undress me."

Brock dropped Freedom's hand and found a seat in a chair near the bed. Ivy gestured to Freedom, with a "come hither". Resistance was futile. Freedom closed the distance between himself and Ivy. She wore a simple, black, form fitting dress and black patent leather stilettos. Freedom mimicked Ivy's earlier action and walked around her. He found the zipper and gently lowered it revealing her naked skin underneath. Freedom eased the dress from her shoulders and peeled it down her body. Ivy extended her hand and Freedom obliged, allowing her to step out of the dress. He was not so careless as to let the dress drop to the floor. Ivy took note and liked that. The only thing left to remove was her shoes as Ivy had on no underwear. Freedom knelt to remove them, but Ivy stopped him.

"Leave them on."

Freedom followed her instructions and stood to his feet. He felt the beginnings of arousal as he appreciated the beauty of her nakedness. Ivy walked away from him and over to the bed. She positioned herself in the middle, upright; one legged crossed gingerly over the other. Brock took his cue and walked over to Freedom. Kissing him lightly on the lips, Brock undressed Freedom. When Freedom tried to return the favor, Brock stopped him.

"No, just you," he whispered. He smiled. It was infectious. Once Freedom was completely unclothed, Brock returned to his seat. Freedom turned to Ivy waiting for permission to approach. He instinctively felt the need to do that. Ivy uncrossed her legs and opened them, pulling her knees up. That was his invitation. Freedom moved to the bed that was high off the floor. He approached from the foot end and maneuvered himself between her legs. He kissed and nibbled her up one leg and down the other, pausing at her hot box just long enough to kiss it lightly. Ivy watched him try to please her. The deference and respect he showed was endearing. She fingered her taut nipples as he returned up the inside of her thigh to pleasure her pussy.

Freedom was no stranger to pleasuring a woman. Early in his sexual life, he had been with women because that's what he was supposed to do. He appreciated the softness of a woman, but realized that he also liked the firmness of a man. He had both, singularly and enjoyed them. The prospect of having both together with Brock and Ivy enticed him. He desired to satisfy Ivy fully, so he would be welcomed with open arms to their twosome.

Freedom fingered the folds of Ivy's puss and found her pearl. He replaced his finger with his tongue and toyed with it, licking and flicking it with his tip. Ivy lifted her hips so his tongue pressed against her sweet spot more firmly. She gyrated on his face, continuing to squeeze and thumb her nipples. Freedom's member hardened. The first of her female warmth oozed onto his tongue and he lapped it up. By this point, Brock had his pants unzipped, with one leg over the arm of the chair stroking his exposed cock. Ivy lowered her hips onto the bed, released her breasts and pulled Freedom's hair lifting his face from between her thighs. Leaning forward, she pushed Freedom back so he lay on the bed. Freedom's head hung slightly off the king-sized bed. Balancing expertly on her heels, Ivy mounted his erect dick. As she enveloped his cock into her wet pussy, her vaginal muscles squeezed and released his shaft as she gradually slid her way down.

Freedom's eyes rolled to the back of his head as her hot womanhood engulfed his nine inches of broad manliness. Ivy didn't waste time by fucking him slow. She took his fullness in all the way to the hilt and rocked back and forth titillating her G spot with his stiff dick. He raised himself up, the sensation overwhelming him, and grabbed Ivy around the waist. Her pussy convulsed as he filled every corner of her jewel. Freedom kissed her full lips. She tasted herself in his mouth. Ivy liked the way she tasted and her puss pulsed against his firmness. She bounced softly on his cock causing increased friction between them. Freedom tongued her deeply relishing in the feeling. Ivy pulled away from the kiss and gingerly bit his bottom lip. The slight sensation of pain egged his fuck on. Ivy released his lip, leaned back and used his legs to brace herself. The arch of her back changed the angle of her pussy and Freedom's cock throbbed inside her. Releasing her waist, he took both of her luscious breasts into his hands and suckled on one nipple then the other. Ivy grinned and allowed a slight

143

laugh to escape her lips. She allowed him to feast at her bosom all the while increasing the intensity of her downward thrusts.

She wanted more. Ivy took him deep with every stroke and rode him vigorously. Freedom returned every downward stroke by pushing into her; his feet planted firmly against the bed. The wetness of her pussy slapped against his caramel thighs. The sound was as intoxicating as the motion itself. Brock loved what he was seeing. Ivy clearly approved of his choice for her. Watching his lover fuck his lover made Brock's dick even harder. He wanted in. He wanted Ivy to invite him in. Mid stroke, Ivy stopped. Her jewel held just the tip of Freedom's cock. She smiled down at him. Freedom was everything Brock said he would be. He wasn't afraid to let himself go, to fully immerse himself and give of himself fully. She saw he was vulnerable to her prowess and it pleased her. Freedom was so enthralled in the way she fucked him, it caught him off guard when the sensation stopped. He lifted himself onto his elbows to see why things stopped midstream.

"Come get what you want," Ivy purred. She was such a fuckin' tease and Freedom loved it. Supporting himself with his hands on the bed, he pushed up into her warmth. This time she gave nothing back. He had to work for it. Reach for it. Show himself worthy to touch her there. Freedom was up to the task and reached the height of her with every upward motion. Using his arms for balance and his legs for support, he managed to raise up and cradle Ivy, pushing deeply into her and then bending his elbows and knees just enough to push in again. They found syncopation there and the walls of Ivy's hot box moistened his stiff cock again.

Ivy placed both her hands on Freedom's chest and eased him back down to the bed. She spun on his cock, turning her back to him. The new position gave Freedom a new angle of her womanliness to explore and he fully intended to do so. Her full ass bounced against his abs as she used his knees to brace herself. On the verge of exploding, Freedom sat up and wrapped his arms around Ivy's waist slowing her fast-paced motion down to a slow grind. He wanted to feel every corner of her warmness and bring her to a higher level of ecstasy. Ivy put her arms over her head and pulled Freedom's head into her. Her slightly arched back pushed her breasts into prominence and Freedom fondled them as he kissed her neck. Ivy wanted more. As she slow fucked Freedom, she called Brock to her.

He stood to his feet and took off the rest of his clothes. He approached the bed. Freedom noticed him and smiled. He was glad Brock was invited. Kissing Ivy first and then Freedom, Brock climbed into the bed with his erect shaft standing strongly out in front of him. Ivy's eyes gave him permission and he lifted his cock into her awaiting mouth. She kissed the tip and he guided himself in. She sucked him, recreating the rhythm on Brock's member that she and Freedom had achieved. Brock laced his fingers behind Ivy's head and pulled her into him. The totality of his manliness disappeared inside her. Freedom fucked Ivy more intensely as he watched her suck the cock he so enjoyed.

"Shit..." It was all good to Freedom. He'd never had it this way before. Brock turned him on. Ivy was turning him out. It was nirvana. Now Brock wanted more as the veins in his dick pulsed under Ivy's touch. She knew him all too well. Brock moved away from her and helped lift her from Freedom's clutches. Ivy got on her knees in front of Brock and he mounted her from behind. He loved that pussy and began to pound it with intensity. It was now Freedom's turn to observe. Lying immediately in front of Ivy, he manhandled his cock keeping his erection as Brock pounced in the pussy. He wasn't left out for long. Ivy reached for his cock. Before obliging, Freedom kissed her, took her tongue fully into his mouth and tasted Brock on her lips. The intermingling of the two tasted good to him. Freedom got on his knees in front of her. She took him in; the inside of her mouth feeling as warm as her jewel box. Once again, without effort the three fell into a succinct rhythm; moans and groans escaping each of their lips. Ivy's vocalizations reverberated against Freedom's cock.

"I wanna cum so bad, oh my God," Freedom exhaled. Ivy stopped her suck and pushed Freedom back.

"No, I'm not done with you yet." She looked over her shoulder at Brock who was still slow grinding her puss. "We're not done with you yet." Like an unspoken agreement between the two of them, Ivy lifted herself from Brocks engorged member. Freedom's eyes fell there. He wanted Brock too. He restrained himself, willing his climax to subside. He didn't want to be done either.

Ivy sat momentarily on the bed and fingered her pussy with one and hand and stroked Freedom's cock with the other. He didn't want to disappoint her by shooting his hot gism on her hand so he steeled himself against the seduction of her touch.

147

Brock climbed off the bed, stopping briefly at the side table to get a condom. Strapping up, he moved over to the bed. Brock kissed Ivy and laid her back on the bed. He pulled her legs up and plunged his covered cock into her. She moaned. Satisfied the prophylactic was sufficiently wet, he let her legs down. Ivy got back near the middle of the bed on all fours. Taking Freedom's hand, she guided him behind her between herself and Brock.

He didn't need to be told what to do. He'd been waiting for this. Freedom guided himself into Ivy's wetness. It was like being home. His cock throbbed desperately. Brock, still standing, leaned Freedom slightly forward and fingered Freedom's asshole. Taking both hands, he spread Freedom's ass cheeks and guided his thickness into Freedom. Freedom slowly pushed back onto Brock until his ass touched Brocks' strong thighs. He brought Ivy with him; his cock touching the pearl at the top of her pussy. The three remained still; the only movement was from the throbbing of each of their sex tools.

"Keep still, we got this," Brock told Freedom. Brock reached down and lifted Freedom's arms until they were over his head. He bent down so Freedom's hands could lace behind his head. The highness of the bed made it easier. Ivy's pussy muscles squeezed and released Freedom's dick and he felt the throbbing fullness of Brock inside him. Then, she slowly started to push against Freedom's cock, which pushed Brock deeper into Freedom. Brock laced his arms underneath Freedom's and braced him for what was to come. Ivy moved her hips back more forcefully relishing the fullness Freedom offered her. Freedom's internal heat rose as he experienced the push and push of the two he lay with. Ivy never sped up, but her grind on Freedom's cock intensified. Brock's thick cock found greater depths from the action Ivy initiated.

And then it was Brock's turn. Ivy felt the shift as Brock fucked Freedom with intention. He allowed Freedom's hands to fall and as Freedom went forward, Brock placed his hands on Freedom's back. Every thrust Brock delivered pushed Freedom deeper into Ivy. Now Freedom laced his arms underneath Ivy's, cupping her shoulders. Brock rocked Freedom rhythmically angling the curve of his cock to penetrate deeper into the inner sides of Freedom's ass. Bending slightly at the knee, Brock pushed all of himself into Freedom's cavity and ground his hips in circular motion. Ivy echoed Brock's actions on Freedom's cock, grinding her pussy into him and covering his cock to the hilt.

Freedom's ball sack rubbed against the front of Ivy's vagina filling them both an intense new sensation. Freedom gasped. He'd never been fucked so intensely before. Loving how he made his new lover feel, Brock lifted onto his tip toes pushing his thick cock to the highest height he could reach inside Freedom. At that moment, Freedom almost lost it.

But neither Brock nor Ivy were quite done. Brock firmly grabbed Freedom by the hips and moved his cock from side to side. It was like a domino effect; his cock reciprocating in Ivy's spasming jewel. The heat between them rose. Ivy felt Freedom's cock contract and throb harder.

"Not yet, Freedom, baby. Not yet... I want more..."

Ivy eased herself off Freedom. Brock eased himself out of Freedom as well. Brock removed his condom and grabbed another one handing it to Freedom. He wasn't sure what was to happen next, but he was willing to do whatever they wanted him to. Ivy laid on her side.

"Get it wet," Brock instructed Freedom as he lay down in front of Ivy leaving Brock positioned behind her. Ivy lifted her leg straight into the air. Taking a cue from Brock's earlier maneuver, Freedom eased his cock into Ivy's pussy. Brock fingered her clit as Freedom fucked her. Ivy's wetness lathered the condom. Brock halted Freedom's stroke with his hand and helped guide his enveloped cock to Ivy's second hole. Ivy lifted her ass cheek to accommodate Freedom's pulsating cock. This was new for Freedom. He was used to receiving anal, but had never given it to anyone. He liked the way Ivy's tight ass hole felt against his hard cock.

Brock tongue kissed Ivy and eased his cock into her pussy. Releasing her ass cheek, Ivy pulled her leg back further to accommodate the both of them. Separating from Ivy's lips, Brock leaned forward as did Freedom. They kissed intensely, their tongues dancing. Freedom slid his arms underneath Ivy and cupped her breasts as Brock sucked her nipples and tongue teased Freedom's fingers. Ivy squealed with pleasure that sent both men on a mission to completely satisfy her. Again, the agreement between parties was unspoken. Brock moved with intention inside Ivy's pussy. Freedom matched each stroke deep in her ass. They used whatever they needed to as leverage.

"Yes, fuck me gottdammit!! Fuck all of me..."

The strokes between the two men alternated from staccato to deep long thrusts. Ivy reached one peak after the next. Her pussy showered Brock's schlong with wetness and kept her ass hole moistened for Freedom.

"Please, can I cum inside you," Freedom begged breathlessly.

The squeeze of her canal around his dick, Brock's cock just inches from his, the whole experience was more than Freedom could handle anymore. He had to release. He had to let it go before he internally combusted.

"Yes, baby, cum for, Ivy…"

Freedom was grateful. He eased his pounding cock from her ass and removed the condom. He looked to Brock who willingly obliged. Freedom inserted no sooner than Brock removed himself.

"Ahhhh… you feel so damn good, Ivy… damn, damn, damn…" He pounded her flesh fast and furious, his balls smacked loudly against her ass. Ivy kept Brock's member hard by fisting it slowly with both hands.

And then Freedom exploded inside her wetness. His body shivered as his gism lathered the insides of her vaginal walls.

"That's right, baby, give it all to mama."

His rhythm slowed as he emptied himself into her.

"What about me," Brock asked his cock still rock hard. Ivy released him. As he continued to lie inside Ivy's warmness, Freedom took Brock's cock in his hand and guided its fullness into his mouth. With one hand, Brock cupped Freedom's head as he fucked his mouth.

"Grrrr..." The animalistic growl from Brocks lips coincided with the hot shot of cum that coated the back of Freedom's throat. Freedom didn't allow one drop of the thick liquid to escape his lips. He swallowed all of what Brock gave him. When the last drop was licked from his tip, Brock collapsed on the bed next to Ivy. Freedom's cock continued to throb inside her jewel. Her warmness gave him life. The three of them smiled warmly at each other and kissed passionately, one between the other. Freedom then rested his head on Ivy's belly as Brock cradled her in his strong arms; their legs comfortably intertwined. Even in all of the bliss Ivy found herself in, she still missed Assent. She lay with Freedom and Brock and thought about her.

That encounter was the first of many. Freedom was welcomed into the fold with open arms. He fell in love with both of them. Things were better than good. For a long time, they were great.

It was more than just great sex between Ivy and Freedom. She was a master practitioner and he was a willing student. Ivy gave Freedom insight into who he was as a man. That was different for him. Although Freedom was masculine and to look at him, you wouldn't know him to be attracted to men, in most gay relationships he was the receiver, rarely if ever the giver. With Ivy, he could give. And she let him give until there was nothing left. Ivy was a strong, fierce woman. Then there was a side to her that was just woman. Of course, he still cared deeply for Brock and nothing was quite like the time they spent together, but it wasn't the same. With Brock, he was on the bottom. He'd never penetrated Brock, not one time in all the times they were together, even when Ivy was present. Freedom enjoyed his new-found vantage point. The few women he did have encounters with in the early part of his sexual life didn't compare to Ivy. They were elementary. Ivy was post-secondary, doctoral.

Things between Ivy, Freedom and Brock were real good for a while. Ivy wanted the three of them to be a family and committed to each other with promises they would only be sexual between the three of them. The newness and variety the relationship offered was appealing to Brock. He was down with it from the beginning. Freedom was happy to have found not one but two people he developed deep feelings for. He was more than willing to become a trio. Not long after their first encounter, Freedom was asked to move in with them. Ivy wasn't a patient woman. She wanted what she wanted when and how she wanted it. They both lived to please her. Freedom readily packed his things and moved into the much larger, much grander home Ivy and Brock shared.

Their bond intensified rather quickly. It was nothing for either of them at any given time to say how much they cared for the other or express their affections for each other. Brock spent time with Ivy separately from Freedom. Ivy spent time alone with

Freedom. Brock and Freedom had their alone time as well. But they always managed to come back together as a trio. That's when things were most exciting, when the relationship was special.

There were never any tiffs between the trio members. There were disagreements of course, but the rule was never to go to bed angry. They adhered to the rule. Ivy would have it no other way. But there was definitely no set rule about sleeping arrangements. You kind of ended up where you ended up. Ivy wouldn't have that any other way either. Ivy occupied the master bedroom and Brock and Freedom had their own bedrooms. Recently, Ivy started spending quite a bit of alone time with Freedom. Several nights in a row Brock found himself alone in his room while the two of them occupied the master bedroom. Ivy never slept in either of their rooms. If one or the both of them were to be with her, it would be in the master. Initially it didn't bother Brock. Freedom and Ivy were together like this before, one to two nights in a row. This time, however, the two were together nearly a week with not so much as an invitation for Brock to join them.

Brock tried to act like it was no big deal. He lay in his bed at night alone, hearing the sounds of passionate love making down the hall. Brock knew

Ivy. She was like a double-edged sword. To love her was dangerous. To not love her was equally as dangerous particularly once she claimed you as her own. But Freedom? Brock expected more from him than that. Freedom was his dirty little secret. Freedom was his lover he thought was more gay than straight. He didn't expect Freedom to fall for her so easily or so quickly. Hell, Brock brought Freedom to the party! He owed him some level of loyalty and some lovin'. He had to chuckle because he knew better than most, that Ivy had a way with people. Freedom really didn't stand a chance against the feminine wiles of Ms. Ivy Frances Renee Sims. Deep down inside, he knew that to be true, but it didn't excuse how he felt about Freedom. The animosity was building.

The sexually tinged sounds from the master bedroom grew louder. There was no way Brock couldn't hear them even if he tried. *I should invite my own motherfuckin' self in, shit... What they gone tell me? No?* Brock thought to himself as he lay in the dark wearing only his boxers. His manhood responded to the sounds he overheard. His imagination wandered wildly because he knew how both of them got down. But he was the Alpha Male, not Freedom. Freedom was soft, a bottom boy. *He don't lay pipe like me... what the fuck is Ivy thinkin'?*

Brock resisted the temptation to crash the party. He'd angered Ivy one time before and he never wanted a repeat of that scenario. She could be vicious. He much preferred the softer side of Ivy, so no, he didn't knock on the door. That would be suicidal... *Shit, she'll be back... you can best believe that... I'll get her back...*

Chapter Twelve

...missing her...

Assent did her best to get on with her life, but that was hard to do after encountering the force that was Ivy Sims. Ivy came into Assent's life just when she needed her most. Assent was flailing, unfocused and unclear on the kind of love she wanted in her life when Parker offered her to Ivy. Assent was fond of Parker and the two of them were good together, but they were just good. There were no rockets shooting off, or dynamic explosions when the two of them were together. There were no fireworks, physically or emotionally. Parker was nice, but she was simple, too simple for Assent. Even though some would have been offended by being offered up to another person as a bribe, if you will, Assent thanked Parker for gifting her to Ivy. Being with Ivy made Assent consider whether she was being gifted or whether she received one.

Assent craved an intellectual equal and a sexual prowess. Ivy was both. Even though some would see Ivy as cocky and overly confident, Assent saw her quiet strength. She never boasted or bragged. People were drawn to Ivy. She never had to give chase. Braggadocios people couldn't draw flies to the buttermilk like Ivy could. And Assent was drawn in even though she walked away. At times, Assent regretted her decision to leave instead of staying and talking to Ivy, to try and get her to understand, to open up. Other times, Assent felt she made the right decision, the only decision she could make given the fact that Ivy stayed closed off from her.

Still, there were moments, much like this one, when Assent missed Ivy desperately. She considered reaching out to her, but Assent knew that to be a no, no. That would make Assent look needy, desperate. That would be a huge turnoff to Ivy. If she didn't reach out though, she would have to wait and hope Ivy reached out to her; that maybe Ivy actually missed her too and would send the text Assent longed for. Assent considered trying to move on, to give another woman a chance to win her heart, but she knew herself better than anyone else. Assent knew regardless of the amazing traits and characteristics another woman possessed, she would immediately compare that woman to Ivy to see if she measured up. Inevitably, that woman would not which made Assent miss Ivy even the more. That could turn into a vicious cycle of inviting and rejecting that Assent really didn't want to be bothered with.

On the other hand, who was Ivy to have her waiting in the wings? Assent was an amazing woman in her own right. She was accomplished, self-sufficient, and independent. Why should she wait for some random text with only a time stamp to signal when she would be allowed to re-emerge into the life of the woman her heart desired most? Assent was too much of a woman to be put on the back burner if she was on the burner at all... she hoped she was... Assent wasn't totally ready to give up on Ivy. They could be good, no, so great together. Assent wanted one more chance to crack through Ivy's heavy armor and win her heart. So, she would wait. She would wait and send out positive energy into the universe she hoped would be returned with a text from Ivy.

Brock had a long, trying day at work. It was late, very late when he returned home. Rush hour traffic had died down hours before and Brock was grateful for the nearly empty roads. He could get home faster that way. The deadline for the project he was currently working on was fast approaching and his team was falling behind. The level of frustration he felt was palatable and he couldn't wait to get out of the office, loosen his tie, get in his car and get the hell away from there for a while. Brock needed a release and he knew just how to get it. He thought about the night before, the night he spent alone as his two lovers spent time together. Brock intended to rectify that. He would have them both.

Brock pulled up to the three-car garage, hit the button, and waited for the garage door to completely ascend. His spot was open and both Freedom and Ivy's cars were there. He smiled. His plans were working out. Brock pulled his Mercedes 450SL in, turned off the ignition, grabbed his briefcase and made his way toward the door that led into their sprawling home. Hitting the garage door button on the wall to close things up, he proceeded down the hallway that led into the kitchen. The heels of his Stacey Adams clicked against the travertine tiles.

"… sssss… ah… ah… ah…"

He heard them before he saw them. Rounding the corner, Brock Stopped cold in his tracks. Strewn clothes blocked contact between his shoe and the hard floor. He saw Ivy. He saw Freedom. Ivy's hands gripping the edge of the granite countertop braced her body midair. Her legs were wrapped around Freedom's waist and he held her suspended. Freedom's cock was deep in Ivy's hotbox and the pounding he was giving her was audible. If there was background noise, Brock couldn't hear it. The only sound he heard was the sound of the two of them fucking.

Neither noticed Brock standing there as Ivy rode Freedom's dick. Freedom moved further underneath her. Ivy's arms no longer bore any weight and she wrapped them around Freedom's neck as he continued to fuck her without mercy. She kissed him feverishly and his stroke slowed. He thrusted hard and deep lifting Ivy with each one.

Her head fell back, disengaging their lips and she gasped in ecstasy; her love juices mixing with his as he unleashed his load deep inside her walls. Brock stood silent. Ivy held Freedom lovingly, until his body no longer shook from the climactic heights they'd just reached. Freedom held her tight, kissing her neck. He looked up to see Brock standing there. Freedom smiled. He was always glad to see his lover. Brock's affect was flat and unresponsive.

Brock crossed the room without acknowledging either of them. The sound of his shoes clacking against the floor returned. It was the first Ivy noticed of someone else being there. She was unfazed. There was no reason for her to be.

Brock was fuming. He stomped up the stairs like a tantrumming child. Getting to his bedroom, he slammed the door and tossed his briefcase on the bed. What was he so angry about? Why did seeing Freedom and Ivy together piss him off so? Isn't that the arrangement they made so many months ago? Neither of them broke the rules of the relationship so why did it bother Brock so? But Brock was not in the head space to be rational and reasonable. For whatever reason, he felt he was wronged somehow, cheated. Flopping on the bed, Brock held his head in his hands and sulked.

Freedom followed Ivy up the stairs, her naked body glistening from their intense encounter. She planned to take a shower. Freedom wanted to see Brock. The two parted at the top of the stairs, Ivy headed to the master and Freedom down the hall to see his man. He tapped lightly on the door and waited for Brock to respond. None of the three were big into locking doors or ultra-privacy. They lived openly with each other so there was no need for the kinds of restraints that some chose to live by. There was no response from the other side. Freedom knew he was there and rapped lightly on the door again, this time turning the handle and peaking inside. He saw Brock sitting on the bed; shoulders slumped with his head in his hands.

Freedom entered the room and made his way to Brock. He hoped nothing was wrong. It wasn't like Brock to walk away like he did downstairs without as much as a 'hello' or better yet, joining in on what Freedom and Ivy had going on. That would have been Freedom's preference. He missed Brock and desired to spend some one on one time with him.

"You okay, Babe," Freedom asked kneeling down immediately down in front of Brock on the carpeted bedroom floor. Brock was unresponsive.

"Something happen? Did you have a hard day?" Brock still didn't respond. Instead he flopped back on the bed and fixed his eyes on the ceiling. Part of Brock knew his anger and frustration were irrational. The other part of him felt justified in his feelings. There was also a certain level of shame in being a jealous lover. He brought this situation on himself really, agreeing to it because his lady asked him to. But who was he to deny Ivy anything. That mixed bag of feelings was a part of Brock's silence.

"I can make you feel better," Freedom suggested placing a hand firmly on Brock's thigh. The touch felt good, but Brock didn't acquiesce verbally. His body defied his silence. Freedom took Brock's silence as a sign of approval. Freedom lifted himself up enough to reach Brock's belt buckle which he quickly opened. Unzipping Brock's pants with one hand, Freedom used the other to push the opened trousers aside. Freedom inserted his hand into the fold of Brock's boxers and found his semi erect penis; finding his treasure already responding pleased Freedom.

"I missed you too, bae," he cooed as he stroked Brock's cock to greater life. Brock held firm his resolve despite the sexual ache he desperately wanted to remedy. Freedom pulled Brock's manhood free from the confines of the boxers and continued to stroke it to hardness. Sure, he was just with Ivy, but there was something about a long, strong cock that turned him on. He felt the urgency in his on manliness grow as he leaned in, kissed and licked the tip of his lover's pole.

Brock kept his eyes fixed on the ceiling and mentally tried to steel himself against the physical pleasure he was receiving. It had been a while since he'd been touched by either of his lovers and he missed the connection only intimacy provided. Still, he was angry and wanted to stay that way. But damn Freedom's mouth felt so good...

Freedom didn't want to keep his lover restrained. He reached on both sides of Brock's hips and eased his pants down. At first Brock offered no assistance. Freedom thought he was being coy, so he deep throated Brock's cock in one fail swoop and massaged the tip in the back of his throat. Without conscious, Brock lifted his hips loving the sensation. His resistance was futile and when Freedom released Brock's dick from his mouth, Brock put his hands to his sides and started the motion of pushing his pants down without rising from the bed. Freedom took it from there, pulling Brock's pants and underwear past his knees and to the floor. He stopped long enough to remove Brock's shoes so he could totally remove any physical inhibitors.

The absence of Freedom's mouth around his cock caused Brock to notice the coolness of the room. He longed for warmth, the warmth of his lover. He dared not ask for it or encourage it. That would be weak. Brock didn't want to give in, not yet. As if reading Brock's mind, Freedom wasted no time in returning to Brock's manhood. He kissed and nibbled Brock's inner thigh working back up to his prize. Freedom pushed Brock's legs open and fondled his balls; taking one then the other in his mouth. Brock fought to keep his body still, to offer no response to Freedom's actions. Freedom was not deterred though. Turning his mouth sideways, he sucked and licked the base of his lover's dick and fingered the tip. A deep moan grew in Brock's throat, but he squelched it. Freedom licked the underside of Brock's manhood from bottom to top. He pushed his tongue into the hole at the tip and licked the curve.

Freedom's hardness grew as he deep-throated Brock again, squeezing and releasing Brock's schlong as he sucked his length. Brock found it hard to resist. As if overcome with feeling, Brock sat up and placed both hands behind his lover's head. He pushed his thickness into Freedom's wanton mouth and the two fell into a familiar rhythm that set both of their bodies ablaze with desire.

"Mmm, mmm, mmm..." Brock grunted with every thrust. He missed his man and was mad he felt such strong feeling for him. Freedom took every thrust Brock had to offer and his reaction told Brock he wanted more. Freedom moaned deeply. Brock thrust faster and harder holding Freedom's head firmly. Freedom squeezed Brock's hips pulling his lover into him more. Brock almost shot his wad, but stopped short releasing Freedom's head and palming his lover's forehead encouraging his dick's release. Freedom looked up into Brock's eyes. They connected. Freedom smiled. He fully released Brock from his lips and eased back sitting on his knees.

Brock got up from the bed and stood Freedom to his feet. Freedom palmed the back of Brock's head and pulled him close making Brock kiss him; their hardened cocks being pushed against the other's body. When Brock showed some resistance, Freedom licked Brock's lips seductively. Brock, still holding on to the remnants of his earlier feelings grabbed Freedom by the shoulders and pushed him down on the bed. Freedom liked it when Brock strong armed him. It was like a tortured erotic dance between the two. Still naked from his earlier rendezvous with Ivy, Freedom scooted back from the edge of the bed making room for his lover. Brock climbed on the bed on his knees and Freedom placed his legs on top of them. Brock didn't care about a condom or nothing else. He wanted, needed to be inside Freedom.

Freedom lifted his cock with one hand and his ball sack with the other as Brock guided his firmness into Freedom's ass. It felt so damn good to Brock, but he didn't let Freedom know that, not with words. He coerced the canal to open as he pushed in and pulled back, pushed in and pulled back; his cock inching in further and further.

Brock thrust deeper, putting the fullness of his body weight into his stroke. Freedom lifted his legs and placed one on each of Brock's shoulders. He wanted to be fully available to his man lover. Brock wrapped his arms around Freedom's legs as he fucked his ass hole. Freedom stroked his own cock. His hardness grew with pressure. Brock was resolute as his man pole disappeared into Freedom. Brock's balls flapped against his lover's upturned ass. He watched as Freedom stroked his own cock with both hands matching Brock stroke for stroke. Freedom took his finger and touched the pre-cum emerging from the tip. He offered his finger to Brock and he hungrily licked and sucked Freedom's finger dry. Brock hated himself for it. Freedom smiled. The tortured dance continued. Brock looked into Freedom's eyes intensely as his dick pulsed hard inside his canal. Freedom returned Brock's unwavering gaze. Their connection was undeniable, even for Brock.

"Yes, baby, yes," Freedom moaned with pleasure. He lifted his legs from Brock's shoulders and spread them wide his feet high on the bed near his ears. Freedom's ass was more upturned. The elevated shift gave Brock new access and he pushed deeper into Freedom. The feeling was crazy and Brock's legs shook from the intensity. He placed a hand on the back of Freedom's upturned thighs and used them as leverage. Freedom released his cock and held his legs so Brock could take what he wanted from him. And he did. Brock languished inside his lover, feeling every nuance of Freedom's depth. Brock momentarily let himself go and allowed himself to emotionally connect with his lover and what Freedom offered him. Their eyes met and Brock could see how much Freedom cared about him, wanted him, loved him.

But this is not what this escapade was supposed to be about. He was mad at Freedom and wanted to punish him for wronging him. Brock snapped out of the feeling place and refocused his energy. He couldn't do what he felt he needed to do facing Freedom. It was hard to be angry when his lover was showing him with every look just how much he cared. Brock slowed his stroke and then stopped. He lifted himself out of Freedom and stood up. Freedom wasn't about to let the good feelings end. He lowered his legs and stood up facing Brock. Brock was not going to succumb to another passionate kiss. He didn't give Freedom the chance. Instead, he took Freedom by the waist and turned him so he faced the bed.

Freedom looked over his shoulder and smiled at Brock as he climbed onto the bed. Brock moved up immediately behind him and spread Freedom's ass cheeks apart. Freedom's cock throbbed and he stroked it firmly as Brock mounted him.

"Oh, God, I missed you, Brock, yes baby, oh yes," Freedom said as he pushed back against Brock's hardness. He fisted his own cock harder as he felt his cavity opening up again to his lover. Brock concentrated on the fuck, not giving in to Freedom's sultry words. He rocked Freedom back and forth inching his cock deeper in.

"Come on, Bae, give me what I've been missing. Please, Brock, give it to me..."

Brock hated how good being inside Freedom felt. He pushed deeper until Freedom's ass cheeks lay against his thighs. The tight cavity enveloped Brock's dick and he held one ass cheek in each hand pushing upward so that Freedom's asshole stretched taut. Brock fucked Freedom deeply without speaking. He concentrated all his energy, thoughts and feelings into each elongated push his cock made. The slow fuck turned Freedom on and he rolled his hips in figure eights rocking on the tip of Brock's cock for maximum penetration. The increased sensation spent Brock and he groaned.

"Son of a bitch," Brock uttered as Freedom's motions got the better of him. Freedom made him feel so damn good. As Brock's angst grew, his thrusts grew stronger.

"Fuck me, Brock, fuck me," Freedom begged.

Brock's cock contracted as if his lover's words controlled him. Brock's stroke quickened and Freedom matched each push with a push back plunging Brock's cock deeper.

"Mmm, mmm, mmm, mmm," Brock grunted louder as his stroke became faster and faster. The syncopated beat between the two of them increased as Brock pounded Freedom's ass hole harder and faster. Freedom stroked his own cock harder and faster.

"Motherfuckin' son of a bitch," Brock uttered as his thighs tensed from the brewing pressure waiting to emerge from his cock. He fucked Freedom with reckless abandon, his body writhing with sweat. It was like he was entranced, pounding furiously into Freedom's flesh. Brock held Freedom's waist so tight his fingerprints would be there long after the fuck was done. Brock had never been quite so aggressive with Freedom before and for a moment what was pleasure-filled became painful as Freedom's rectum started to tear and burn from the force. But Brock didn't stop. He moved his hand so that both hands rested on Freedom's left side. Brock shifted slightly so that his cock pounded Freedom's canal in the opposite direction, making the distance shorter.

"Mmm, mmm, mmm, gottdamn, son of a bitch, mmm, motherfucka, mmm, mmm, mmm," Brock uttered between clenched teeth. Beads of sweat dotted his forehead as he put in work caving in to his demons. Brock was merciless. The words he uttered rushed from his lips as his internal pressure mounted. Freedom had no words. His mouth was agape and his eyes widened with every thrust. Freedom no longer held his dick. Instead he clawed the bed linens holding on. There was pleasure even in the pain and he wanted Brock regardless.

"Brock, Brock, cum for me, Baby, please! Cum for me, I want you to cum for me, Bae, please, please," Freedom said breathlessly. It was as if they'd transcended to another plane, the two of them locked in an emotionally and physically gripping entanglement. The feeling was mind blowing and they both teetered on the edge of reality. Freedom grabbed his cock again and stroked it vigorously as he held on to his climax. He wanted to cum with his lover and he knew Brock was close, so very close. Freedom completely let go and let himself feel everything. There was no protection from the overwhelming intoxicating wave of sexual satisfaction he felt. Although he would never admit it, Brock reached a level of satiation he'd never felt before. The pace of his fuck increased faster than the ticking of the second hand on a clock. He couldn't take it anymore, he had to cum.

"Ahhhhhhhh," the sound was long, guttural and full of every emotion Brock felt. Freedom lost his breath as his own hot gism screamed from his penis. They stayed that way in suspended animation, losing all touch with reality, but still being grounded to that heightened feeling. It was everything...

They were both spent. All they could do was collapse. They stayed that way with no words exchanged. Freedom's heart was beating out of his chest. Brock stayed inside Freedom until his dick was flaccid. He was emotionally overwhelmed. The two stayed that way for a long time. Eventually, Brock got up from the bed and walked into the bathroom. He still didn't say anything to Freedom. Freedom didn't mind though. He lay there, basking in the glow.

Brock entered the bathroom and locked the door behind him in case Freedom got any ideas. Turning the shower on, Brock leaned against the wall awash with a plethora of feelings he was too worn out to deal with. The bathroom quickly filled with steam and moisture. Brock stepped into the shower and stood under the overhead rain shower allowing the hot liquid to wash over him.

Coming off an amazing high, Freedom found himself alone in Brock's bed. He heard the water running in the bathroom and decided it would be a good idea to get cleaned up too before bed. It had been a long, exhausting yet exhilarating day. A hot shower would top things off nicely. Freedom made his way from Brock's room down the hall to his own room. He remembered his clothes were still sprawled across the kitchen floor and he made a note to get them when his shower was finished.

Freedom finished up his shower and put on a t-shirt and pajama pants; just enough to run downstairs, get his clothes, grab something to drink and get ready for bed. As he exited his room he saw Brock coming out of his room as well. Freedom smiled and waited for Brock near the stairs.

"You left me all alone," Freedom teased smiling from ear to ear. Brock was not in the mood. He still felt some kind of way about everything that happened and didn't really want to deal with Freedom at the moment. Freedom approached him still not picking up on the funky vibe Brock was dishing out. Freedom took his finger and stroked Brock's manhood through his clothes. Brock knocked his hand away forcefully. Freedom was shocked.

"What the hell is your problem, Brock?" The two had an amazing time and Freedom didn't understand where the dis was coming from.

"Just leave me the fuck alone, man," Brock retorted. Ivy heard raised voices outside her bedroom door and made her way into the hallway to see her two men having beef. She leaned against the door jamb and folded her arms across her chest. She wanted to see how it would play out before she intervened. Ivy detected something going on with Brock, but she wasn't going to give him the satisfaction of inquiring. Whatever it was they would have to work it out between themselves. At the end of the day, as long as they continued to make her happy that was all that really mattered to her.

"Brock, don't be like that, I mean…" Freedom's sentiments were cut short as Brock tried to push past him. Freedom wasn't having it and grabbed Brock by the shirt forcing him to deal with the issue.

"Just talk to me, Brock. What's the problem?" There was a whine in Freedom's voice that annoyed the shit out of Brock. *Begging ass motherfucka'*, he thought as he grabbed Freedom's wrists and spun him around. Freedom's back was to the staircase.

"You sorry, bitch ass nigga! Get your gottdamn hands off me! Who the fuck you think you are, pussy ass motherfucka'!" Brock's anger brimmed over. Freedom had never been spoken to that way and he wasn't about to take it unprotested from Brock.

"Motherf-"

At that moment, Brock pushed Freedom with extreme force. Freedom lost his grip on Brock's shirt and he felt himself falling backwards. He grabbed for anything he could catch hold to but there was nothing there but air. Ivy gasped as she saw one of her lovers cascading down the stairs and the other standing there responsible for the melee. Freedom fell head over feet crashing against the casings. His body struck the hardwood stairs multiple times contorting and breaking things not designed to be broken. The sounds of wood meeting flesh echoed in the massive entryway. Freedom tried to stop his descent, but there was a loud snap and things went totally blank.

"What the hell did you do, Brock," Ivy questioned as she moved closer to the stairs. She looked down and saw Freedom's body lying there in a disheveled heap. Brock stood wide eyed at the top unable to readily respond to Ivy's inquiry. He was mad at Freedom true enough, but his intention wasn't to hurt him, not really. Or was it?

"Stupid, Brock, just stupid," Ivy quipped as she descended the staircase to see about Freedom. Brock remained at the top and watched the love of his life attend to another man.

"Freedom? Freedom?" Ivy's appeal was genuine. She didn't want to see anyone hurt and Freedom was obviously hurt. He was still breathing though, shallow, but still breathing. He didn't respond to her.

"Call 911!" Ivy commanded Brock who stood stuck at the top of the staircase. Ivy muttered obscenities under her breath disgusted by Brock's juvenile actions. Ivy looked up to see if Brock was doing what he was told. He stood there stoic, still seemingly unable to move.

"Gottdammit, Brock! Call 911!"

The shrill command in her voice compelled his feet to move. Brock rushed into Freedom's bedroom closest to the sitars and picked up the phone. His hand shook as he dialed the three emergency digits.

"Why did you do it," Ivy asked as she mounted Brock's hardness. He refused to allow conversation about the other to interfere with the present. Brock eased his cock inside her walls and felt her. It had been a while since they were together this way just the two of them and he was not about to waste energy or conversation discussing what didn't matter to him in the least. He wasted no time stroking deep and long. The thickness of his manhood filled her. Brock concentrated on each stroke, relishing in her feminine wiles. He felt some resistance, disengagement from Ivy. Looking up he saw seriousness on her face, not because of his stroke, but because of her question. It was enough to blow his sexual high. Brock put his finger to Ivy's lips, encouraging her to be quiet. Ivy pushed his hand away as she ground down on his cock. He inhaled as the intensity of her touch heightened his sexual craving for more of her.

"Don't... you know better," Ivy said. She balanced herself on her tiptoes and moved her hips up and down on top of Brock who was sitting in an armless chair. Brock didn't want Ivy to withdraw herself from him; he needed to be close to her, inside her too much to risk it. But Freedom was not what he wanted to talk about at a time like this. Ivy was insistent.

"I asked you a question and I expect an answer." She pressed down on his erection fast, down to the hilt and then quickly lifted herself. Ivy dangled her

181

wet puss just above his pulsating cock and refused entrance until she got what she wanted.

"Damn, baby, don't do me like that, come on," Brock said almost whining. He wasn't concerned about being manly. He didn't care about looking weak. Brock wanted Ivy and he wanted her unrepentantly. He pushed his hips off the chair trying to reach her treasure. Ivy denied him, lifting higher just outside his reach. Brock grabbed for her hips to limit her mobility and make the kind of contact his hard on craved. Ivy resisted, evading his grasp. She lifted her leg, threatening to abandon him altogether; her gaze defying him to defy her. His eyes pleaded with her to stay.

"Answer the fuckin' question, Brock. I won't ask again." Ivy didn't make her puss available to Brock.

"'Cause of you!" Their proximity was too close for such loud intonations. He really didn't mean to scream. Brock's emotions were all over the place. He could count on Ivy to check him with the quickness.

"Who The hell do you think you're raising your voice to?" Ivy completely stood up and folded her arms underneath her naked breasts.

Brock knew he blew it and his manliness decreased with every second she was away. His desire for her never waned though. Ivy turned her back and started walking out of the room.

"My bad, Ivy, but damn," Brock said moving swiftly behind her. "You was giving him everything. That motherfucka' ain't man enough to replace me." Brock grabbed her shoulder and turned her toward him, another no, no.

"Oh, so now you gone push my ass down the fuckin' stairs?"

Brock released his grasp on Ivy and lifted them both into the air backing off.

"Fuckin' caveman..."

"Ivy, please..." Ivy stepped away from Brock, but continued to face him. She scowled in her signature nice nasty way. Ivy wasn't one to scream or shout. She spoke softly with maximum authority.

"You had a temper tantrum. You were out of order. If you want me happy, you will make this right." Brock didn't lift his head. He was being scolded and he knew to take it. "Don't forget, he could still tell what happened. You don't want that now do you? Then he would have me all to himself while you sit in a fuckin' jail bent over for some stag." Ivy sashayed away and stopped briefly at the entrance to the master bedroom.

"Fix it."

Brock stood there long after she closed the door. He had no real choice but to make it right. He couldn't afford to lose everything. He couldn't afford to lose Ivy.

Chapter Thirteen

… the apology…

Situations had never been this out of control for Ivy before. She blamed herself, even though it was Brock's hands that physically hurt Freedom, it was her choices that pushed him to it… at least that's how she felt when she was alone and things were quiet. Ivy would never openly say any of this to Brock or Freedom for that matter. That wasn't her way. But Brock had better make this right or…

It wasn't a veiled threat. It was something she considered even before Brock fucked up. For Ivy, there was something still missing. That something had a name. She had a name. Ivy missed Assent... Brock was good, Freedom as good, Brock and Freedom, before this, was real good, but it still wasn't exactly what Ivy wanted, what she longed for. Lying across her bed, Ivy reached for the phone. She picked it up and put it down several times. She didn't want to look weak. Ivy didn't want to feel weak. Assent was the one who walked out, she should be the one to make the first move. Thinking about that Ivy had to laugh. Assent was smart. Assent knew if she did that, Ivy would see that as a weakness and a turn off and Ivy wouldn't respond. It would bolster Ivy's ego that Assent wanted to come crawling back to her and Ivy would reject the gesture outright.

No, Assent played this just right. Ivy smiled again. It would take Ivy being the bigger person if the two were to ever connect again. And with all the rampant testosterone in her life, Ivy needed a soft place to land. She picked up the phone again and instead of texting, she dialed Assent's number.

The line cracked and the phone started to ring. Ivy seriously considered hanging up but how lame would that look? The phone rang again. Maybe Assent would be stubborn and not answer. *That could be good,* Ivy thought to herself as the line cracked again.

"Hello."

Her voice was low and sweet, like she was just waking up from a nap in the middle of the day. Ivy hesitated.

Assent waited a second longer and repeated her greeting salutation.

"Hello?"

"Hey, Assent... its Ivy..."

"Hi..."

"Hi..."

Before the call, Ivy thought the conversation would have been awkward but it wasn't. After the first few tense moments, the two eased into a conversation that felt really natural. There were even a few laughs mixed in.

When Assent fell quiet, Ivy found herself a bit unnerved.

"What is it," she asked not sure what Assent's response would be; whether she would cut to the quick and deal with the big ass elephant lurking on the edge of their conversation of whether Assent would keep it light.

Nothin'," Assent replied half-heartedly.

"Don't make me beg, Assent, I don't beg… what's up?" Ivy pressed slightly.

"I was just trying to decide whether to risk it or not."

"Risk what?"

"Risk you dissin' me or pushing me further away," Assent answered her voice getting even softer.

Ivy thought about saying, I wouldn't do that, but she knew that was a lie so she didn't bother.

"Is it worth the risk," Ivy inquired.

"I would like to think so, but I've seen you in action Ivy."

Now there was an awkward and pregnant silence.

"Take the risk. I promise not to bite," Ivy offered.

Assent hesitated.

The line was quiet again.

"I miss you…"

Assent's response was barely above a whisper, but Ivy heard every word. She felt every word.

Silence…

"I miss you too…"

Assent smiled on the other end of the phone…

Brock had to fix it. Ivy gave him no choice. Brock wasn't looking forward to speaking with Freedom, but it was a necessary evil. *Fuckin' bastard probably can't even talk,* he thought to myself as he rode the elevator up to ICU. As the door to the hallway opened, Brock tried to get his shit together. He knew Ivy. He knew how she was. Brock knew how she could be. If he ever wanted to feel that good pussy again, he had to work this out with Freedom.

When Brock opened the door to Freedom's hospital room, there was a nurse in with him taking his dinner tray. When Freedom looked up and saw Brock standing there, a weird look came over his face. Was he scared of Brock? It certainly didn't look like he was glad to see him. Brock waited by the door until the nurse was finished and exited before he walked across the room to the seat by the bed. Brock could tell by the look in Freedom's eyes this wasn't going to be easy.

The whole drive over, Brock thought about what he would say to him, but sitting here with Freedom, just the two of them, was awkward. Ivy was like the buffer between her two boys. She kept things moving. But there was a time before Ivy; a time when Freedom and Brock had a good relationship. That's the shit Brock needed to tap into if this was going to have any chance of working out.

Freedom's eyes remained kind of wide like he was shocked to see Brock, alone. More than that, Brock thought he saw fear. *He's really scared of me*, Brock thought to himself; the realization of how bad he fucked up really sank in.

"Uh, how you feeling, man," Brock asked tentatively, nearly fearing what Freedom's response would be.

Brock had no real expectation of Freedom even speaking, at least that's what the doctor said the last time he visited with Ivy. When Freedom did speak, it caught Brock off guard.

"...o...k..."

It took him a while to get the word out. His voice was low and scratchy. The realization of his ability to speak made Brock think about what Ivy said. If he could speak he could tell. If he told, that shit would be bad for Brock. Playing it off, Brock kept the conversation moving, saying all the shit he went over in his head before he arrived.

"Have they said when you're getting out or are they going to bump you down to a regular floor?"

Freedom put his hand to his chest like it was hard for him to speak. Before he responded he painstakingly reached for the cup of water sitting on the side table. It was taking Freedom too long to get it so Brock handed it to him, trying to expedite the whole process. Freedom's hand shook slightly as he wrapped his fingers around the plastic cup and took a sip through the straw.

"I... don't... know..." he replied after he swallowed. Freedom moved to place the cup back and once again Brock intervened taking it from him and putting it back on the table.

This slow ass conversation was making this shit harder. Brock moved around the bed and across the room to the chair near Freedom. Flopping down, Brock tried to keep things moving, still disengaged, but still trying to protect what he had at home.

Freedom kept staring at Brock with that wide-eyed look. Brock adjusted himself in the seat. This whole conversation was uncomfortable as hell.

"Why..." Freedom's voice was weak and fragmented; contrary to his physical stature.

"Why? Why what," Brock asked finding it hard to hide his irritation.

Freedom was still staring at Brock, but his dark brown eyes were different. There wasn't a wide-eyed look tethered with fear. That fearful look was replaced with challenge. Freedom broke his gaze with Brock long enough to painstakingly look down the length of his body and then back at him.

"Why…?"

When Freedom asked the question this time his voice was a little more forceful, but it still cracked. There was a part of Brock that wished his ass still couldn't speak then Brock could say what he had to say without interruption. Then, Brock could tell Ivy he did what she told him to.

Why was his inquiry pissing Brock off so? It was a logical question, but Brock still wanted to be self-righteous, indignant and angry with Freedom. Brock only came to the hospital because Ivy gave him an ultimatum. Brock didn't want to lose Ivy so he was doing what he had to do.

But there was a major glitch in Brock's whole train of thought and that gaping hole he tried to deny began to rise up in him undeniably. His self-conscious started to raise questions as difficult as the one Freedom posed. And then the real gravity of the situation truly weighed on Brock for the first time. Brock averted Freedom's gaze, not wanting him to see that there was an inner conflict burning up his insides. Was Brock really the kind of dude that let his emotions get so out of control? And if he was, when did he become him?

Brock felt Freedom looking at him, staring right through him. The tension between the two in that moment was more than palatable. Brock could no longer avoid the intensity in which Freedom viewed him. Brock looked up and their eyes met. Brock wanted to look away, to reignite his disdain for Freedom, but the genuineness Brock saw in Freedom's eyes wouldn't let him be so callous. For the first time, Brock paused and looked at Freedom, at what he did, not what Freedom made him do. A single tear fell from Freedom's eye and it pricked Brock's heart, the heart that was so readily steeled against Freedom.

"Why..."

Freedom asked again and this time he broke. The pained inquiry was accompanied by a wave of deep sobs and limitless tears. The body Brock broke quivered, no longer able to contain the agony Freedom's tears so clearly revealed. Brock hung his head in shame. Brock wanted to console Freedom, to tell him it was going to be alright... the irony in that... Instead, Brock sat there with his head hung low, no longer trying to absolve himself of the pain he truly caused. Brock owed Freedom an apology; more than that, Brock owed Freedom an explanation. The naked and unabashed truth of why he acted so rashly.

The room grew silent as Freedom's sobs quieted. Brock started to speak without even lifting his head, feeling ashamed of himself.

"When you asked me why, I tried to act like I didn't understand the question. I did. I knew exactly what you meant. I just didn't want to admit it to myself. Freedom, I'm so very sorry for what I did to you. What I did was inexcusable."

The words spilled from Brock's lips. Even if he wanted to stop them, he couldn't.

"It sounds so stupid now, but I was jealous of you and Ivy. I know it makes no sense, but I was. I let jealousy get the best of me... and you paid the price for it."

The brutal honesty of the words Brock spoke choked him.

"I'm sorry, man. Can you ever forgive me?"

Brock dared to look up to see if Freedom felt the sincerity of his apology. When Freedom stretched out his hand to Brock, he knew Freedom felt his heart. Freedom was a bigger man than Brock ever gave him credit for being. With trepidation, Brock extended his hand as well and took Freedom's into his own. The touch made Brock remember why he was so attracted to Freedom in the first place. There was a gentle tug. Freedom was inviting Brock back in. Brock responded. He lifted himself from the chair and moved to sit on Freedom's bed facing him. Brock wiped the last of the tears that still streaked Freedom's cheeks.

"I'm really sorry…"

Freedom nodded his head and there was a faint smile that parted his lips. Brock wrapped his arms around Freedom and pulled him close. Mission accomplished…

Brock couldn't wait to get home to tell Ivy how good of a boy he was. He was so well trained. He told her all about his visit with Freedom and the fact that Freedom was starting to talk. That let Ivy know it was time for her to make a little visit to the hospital to make sure her other boy was in line.

Brock was eager to accompany Ivy to the hospital. He wanted to make sure his account of what happened matched anything Freedom had to say.

Ivy detested hospitals. It was something about all the sickness and death under one roof that nauseated her. Hopefully, Freedom wouldn't have to be there too much longer and things could return to normal. Ivy didn't know how many more times she could bring herself to come down to that God forsaken place.

After the doctor administered some pain meds to address Freedom's gnawing aches, Brock and Ivy moved closer to the bed and she sat down next to him. He was much calmer now and was able to genuinely smile as Ivy leaned in and kissed his cheek.

"I'm so glad you're feeling better, handsome."

"Yeah, the medicine is really helping a lot."

"I understand you and Brock made nice?" Freedom looked up at Brock and when their eyes connected, Ivy could see Brock told the truth.

"We're good now, right?" Freedom asked Brock.

"Yeah man, it's all good," Brock answered placing a hand on Freedom's shoulder.

"That makes mama very happy. Now, if you play your cards right and remember what I told you, you'll be home before you know it and we can pretend this ugly little situation didn't happen."

Ivy's statement was as much for Brock as it was for Freedom. It was much easier to keep the trio together than for Ivy to start over with new boys that she would have to train.

"I'm so ready to come home," Freedom replied. "I miss you guys so much."

"No worries?" Ivy said. She wanted to make sure her message was clear.

"No worries. I just want to come home," Freedom answered understanding the spoken and implied.

"Excellent."

With that, Ivy leaned in and kissed Freedom on the lips giving him a taste of what he missed. Freedom wrapped his arms around Ivy and pulled her in close kissing her even deeper. Yeah, he missed Ivy. She knew she had nothing to be concerned about.

"See you later, baby."

Ivy got up from the bed and headed to the door. Brock leaned in and gave Freedom a kiss before following behind her. Ivy knew Freedom was smiling from ear to ear. She didn't even need to turn around and see it. Mission accomplished.

Chapter Fourteen

...changing places...

That night, after washing away any remnants of hospital from her body, Ivy crawled into bed and dialed Assent's number. Ever since that first phone call the two spoke nearly every night into the wee hours of the morning. They talked about everything from the weather to politics to religion to the goofiness they saw on television. It was refreshing and new for Ivy, almost like having a BFF. She never had one of those before.

Ivy was getting to know Assent in a way she never intended. But the big pink elephant continued to sit right outside the conversation. Ivy decided it was time to talk about it.

"I know why you walked out."

The statement came out of nowhere. Assent stopped mid-sentence.

"Oh, are we going there," she asked jokingly.

"Yep, let's do it," Ivy joked back.

"Okay."

"Okay."

"So you think you know why I walked out. Well, Ivy Renee Francis Sims, do tell."

"No, do you didn't call me by my full government name."

"Yeah, I did," Assent joked again.

"Hmph, okay, then Assent Mother Earth Johnson," Ivy snapped back.

"That is so not my name," Assent recoiled.

The two enjoyed a hearty laugh.

"So silly," Assent as their laughter started to fade.

"Whateva... but I do know why you left," Ivy said still trying to keep the mood light.

"Tell me."

"Because you so damn nosey.

"What?"

"You heard me, you nosey as hell..."

"Continue," Assent suggested.

"You and I, we never had the conversation," Ivy began.

"And what conversation is that pray tell?"

"The conversation where I tell you the rules of engagement and you agree to them."

"Ah, that conversation."

"Yes, that one. That's a very critical step and we missed it."

"And you think if you would have sat me down and told me the rules, I would have agreed to them without question?"

"Nah, knowing you, there would have been questions," Ivy replied.

"Damn straight," Assent buffed.

"But here's the thing. If we started things off the right way, we wouldn't be where we are right now."

"And how do you figure that?"

"Easy," Ivy began. "Once I told you the rules, you would have made your decision right away, to abide by them or leave and we could have avoided the whole awkward feeling, emotion thing and the walk away."

"What would have been the difference? Me walking away in the beginning or when I did? What's the difference?"

Ivy paused before answering.

"The difference is, I wouldn't have had a chance to care if you walked away in the beginning..."

"Are you saying you care now," Assent pushed.

Ivy was quiet again. *Is this what being vulnerable feels like?*

"Yeah, Assent... I care..."

"Was that so hard?" Assent said teasing.

"Hell yeah." Ivy replied. "But I mean it."

"I know..."

Having Brock and Ivy come to visit Freedom was wonderful. He did genuinely care about both of them and wanted to return to the life they had before 'the situation'. Freedom did believe Brock when he said he was sorry. Freedom wanted to believe Brock meant it. Was he concerned though? Was there a part of Freedom that thought Brock could lose it again? Did Freedom have any anxiety about going back to their situation, to going back 'home'? That's the part of Freedom he struggled to quiet since being in the hospital. Despite Brock's apology, Freedom was angry about how the whole thing played out, but he wasn't willing to give them up, not yet.

Freedom had to be honest with himself. When he got with Brock and Ivy, he completely abandoned his old life. Freedom still worked where he worked before and still affiliated with the same co-workers but on a professional basis only. It was all superficial as Freedom didn't consider any of them to be friends. The friends Freedom did have, he didn't maintain relationship with. Freedom couldn't remember the last time he hung out separate from his new family. He didn't even have a living space to go back to. Freedom left his apartment to move in with Ivy and Brock. They were his life now. They were his friends now. They were his family now. Without them, Freedom felt he had nothing, no place and no one to return to. Even if Freedom had concerns, if let's say Brock was still gunning for him and his apology was less than sincere, Freedom didn't really have a lot of choices. *They're all I have... It has to work out...*

Ivy made some decisions. They weren't easy decisions and Ivy didn't take the choices she was prepared to make lightly. Freedom was nearing time to leave the hospital. Things with Assent were progressing in an unexpected but wonderful direction, and Brock did what he was told to do and made amends. Each one of them served a particular purpose in Ivy's life; they fulfilled a particular role, but Ivy knew the four of them could not peacefully coexist in the same space. Regardless of sexual orientation, the natural proclivity with two men and two women would be the pairing up; two couples residing under one roof. That would not do, not for Ivy. Three was the perfect balance, with Ivy at the center. Any other configuration wouldn't work.

Despite the choice, someone would be hurt. Ivy just had to mitigate the level of hurt. But she was determined to not do what she'd done in the past and cut a person off. She would do it differently this time. More civil, more humane. Maybe she was getting soft? Maybe opening herself up to Assent made her weaken in her resolve? Ivy wasn't sure. The one thing Ivy was certain of is that she had to act on her decision immediately. There was no time to waste.

She waited for him at the kitchen table. Ivy knew Brock would follow the same routine and enter the house from the garage. She thought it best to address him immediately upon entering so there would be no delay. He wouldn't have an opportunity to get comfortable. There was something else Ivy contemplated. Given Brock's jealous rage, she had to consider what he did to Freedom; how he hurt him when Brock felt provoked. Ivy hated to have to think of Brock that way but above all else, Ivy was a realist. When backed into a corner, there was no telling how he might lash out. Being in the kitchen, then, was the best option. She could quickly get her hands on something to protect herself, and make a hasty exit if it came to that.

Ivy hoped it wouldn't though. She hoped there was still mutual respect between the two of them;

that despite what she had to say, he would remain the man she once thought she could live the rest of her life with. Just as expected, Brock arrived precisely on time. She heard the garage door go up and the purr of the Mercedes engine as he parked in the garage. The knob on the kitchen door turned as the garage door closed. Ivy took another sip of the wine she was drinking and braced herself.

Brock entered the kitchen, briefcase in one hand and suit jacket in the other. She waited until he closed the door behind him and put his things down before speaking.

"Hey, babe," Ivy said.

"Hey," Brock replied. "I didn't see you sitting there."

Brock crossed the room to where Ivy sat. He leaned over and kissed her fully on the mouth and then hugged her tightly. The scent of his cologne would linger long after this conversation was over.

"How was it today," Ivy asked adjusting in the chair. Brock's work life was always hectic, but he loved it.

"Man, the folks on this new project are crazy as hell. The team is hanging in there though. We should finish up just before the deadline. So, it's good, it's all good."

Brock crossed the kitchen as he spoke and opened the refrigerator. He reached in and grabbed a beer. He grabbed the open bottle of wine Ivy had been drinking from on his way back to the table.

"Did you have a good day," Brock asked as he freshened her drink.

"It was alright, nothing to speak of."

Ivy hated small talk. Talking about things you didn't really care about was a waste of intellect and words in Ivy's opinion. Brock cracked the seal on his beer and took a long swig.

"Alright, what's up," he asked. He knew Ivy well enough to quickly comprehend that nothing about this situation was right. It felt staged, disingenuine, not like Ivy at all.

"We need to have a conversation."

"I figured as much," Brock replied sitting his bottle down. His demeanor instantly changed and there was a heaviness in his voice. Whatever this conversation was, it wouldn't be good. He felt it.

"We're done."

Brock didn't look at her. Instead, he turned up his beer and finished it off. He sat the empty bottle down hard on the table, unapologetically. Ivy didn't respond.

"That's it?"

"Pretty much…"

Brock pursed his lips and nodded his head slowly, rhythmically, as if there was a song playing in his head. Brock took the empty bottle, laid it on its side, and started spinning it on the table. When he allowed his eyes to look around the kitchen, he noticed for the first time, his bags stacked neatly in the corner. The rhythmic nodding started again.

Ivy crossed her legs under the table, sat back, and waited.

"Care to tell me why, if there's a why?"

Brock paused, but didn't wait for Ivy to respond.

"I mean, I know you. You don't have to have a real reason but if you do, share Ivy…"

"It's time…"

"Time… okay… time like too much time, not enough time, out of time like I didn't make another move fast enough or we only operating on your time?"

Brock's brow furrowed as he continued to spin the bottle. He didn't look up at Ivy. Brock kept his eyes focused on the table.

"It's just time…"

Brock sat back hard in his seat. He sighed deeply as though exacerbated. And then he popped up, as if the chair could no longer hold him and started to pace the floor. Ivy watched him; four paces forward, four paces back, four paces forward, four paces back. Brock ran his hands over his head and then laced his fingers behind his head, elbows extended and walked a few more steps. When he turned and looked at Ivy, she could see a mix of emotions on his face. His eyes were sad but unsettled. She waited. He had more to say. She would allow him the chance to get it off his chest.

"We have been together, like forever... man, I don't believe this... but it's time... okay...anything you ever asked me to do, ever asked me to do, I did it with no problems..."

Then Brock stopped short. He stopped pacing.

"Is this because of that nigga, Freedom?"

Brock came back to the table and placed his hands on the back of the chair, leaning in.

Ivy looked up at him but said nothing.

"Ah okay..." Brock walked away again. This time he leaned his back against the island as he faced Ivy.

"Okay, so because of that li'l situation, you and me gotta be over?"

There really wasn't a question there. Ivy didn't offer an answer.

Brock stared at Ivy like somehow by looking at her, he would get the clarity he sought.

"So you think because of that, I could do something to you, like I would hurt you?"

Ivy titled her head in the opposite direction but didn't speak.

Brock sucked his teeth.

"That's bullshit, Ivy and you know it," he rebuffed. "I ain't never put my hands on you like that, never would... but the fact that you would even think that, about me? Me? Yeah, okay... you know that's fucked up, right?"

Brock turned away from Ivy and leaned heavily against the granite countertop. Ivy got up from the chair and crossed the room. Standing behind him, she wrapped her arms around him and laid her head on the center of his back. Brock's shoulders slumped.

Ivy squeezed him tighter and Brock let her. Slowly he turned to face her. Their eyes locked. She could see the disappointment in his. He could see the resolve in hers. There was no point in any further conversation. Brock had to accept it for what it was. His hands fell casually around her waist and Ivy tenderly kissed his closed lips. Their foreheads touched and they lingered there.

After a few exaggerated moments, Brock broke away from her. He turned and crossed the room to retrieve his bags. As he passed Ivy, she lifted her hand and placed it on his chest. She felt his heartbeat underneath her fingertips. When she dropped her hand, Brock took a decided step toward the door. Ivy didn't turn around, even after she heard the kitchen door close. She heard the engine rev back to life and the garage door open. And then it closed and there was silence. He was gone...

Freedom smiled as the car pulled up to Ivy's place. The driver walked around to his door and opened it. He assisted Freedom in getting to his feet. The walk up to the grand entrance was slow, but Freedom appreciated every step, even though he walked with a cane. It was only temporary though. With hard work and more rehabilitative therapy, his doctors were convinced Freedom would walk assistance free again. Ambient light radiated from the windows of Ivy's spacious home. It was dusk and the street lights were just coming on. The beautiful tree lined street was quiet and now it glowed with a welcoming effervescence. Freedom stood in front of the grand door and rang the bell. He could hear the ringing as it echoed through the house. When the door opened, he smiled as Ivy received him.

"Hey there, handsome," Ivy said as she stepped to the side and allowed Freedom entrance.

He leaned over as he passed and planted a kiss on Ivy's cheek. She closed the door behind him and the two entered the main hall.

Ivy's home was still as nicely appointed as he remembered. There were touches of Ivy everywhere; the facets of her personality reflected in the soft muted color palette with pops of color that drew the eye and caused one to focus, if only momentarily. The look was classic, uncluttered yet warm and inviting. Freedom breathed in deeply and momentarily relished in the moment. He looked around trying to see if Brock was there. He listened, but there were no voices or footsteps other than his and Ivy's.

"Where's Brock?" Freedom asked as he entered the house. Brock hadn't returned to the hospital after his infamous apology. Freedom thought Brock would have picked him up from the hospital, as a good will gesture. Instead, Ivy sent a car for him. Brock was nowhere to be found. He was conspicuously absent.

"He's gone."

Ivy spoke with such finality, Freedom paused to clarify.

"Gone? You mean like gone, gone?"

"Yes, Freedom, gone, gone."

"But I thought..." Freedom began.

"You thought what?"

"I thought you two were together, you know, in a relationship," he replied still not sure what to make of what Ivy was saying.

Ivy snickered.

"'Relationships end, Freedom. That's nothing new."

"I know, but why did it end? I mean, you two have been together for a while..."

"True, but duration doesn't mean it can't end."

"But why though, Ivy?" Freedom knew his questioning placed him on a slippery slope. Ivy could be ruthless and he didn't want to push too hard. But curiosity was getting the best of him.

"He hurt you. I couldn't accept that."

"He apologized though," Freedom offered. Even as he said it, he doubted the sincerity of Brock's words. He doubted Brock's sincerity from the moment he said he was sorry. So why was he still defending him?

"He apologized because I told him too," Ivy said matter of factly.

"I know..."

Instead of going to his bedroom, Ivy led Freedom into the master. Although he was mostly recovered, he still wasn't 100% and Ivy helped him get comfortable in her bed. Ivy sat down on the bed next to him, adjusting the duvet.

"Thank you."

"For what?"

"For sending him away," Freedom continued.

He didn't wait for Ivy to respond.

"I wanted to believe Brock when he apologized to me and there was a part of me that really wanted him to mean he was sorry. I knew him before meeting you and I thought he was a good person. I mean, I really liked him, damn near loved him. But when he lashed out like he did?"

Freedom shook his head as if to shake loose from a bad memory.

"You don't have to thank me. It was time."

"I know I don't have to thank you, Ivy. I want to thank you. If I couldn't trust Brock's apology to be real, there was no way I could come back. And I wanted to come back. I needed to be able to come back to you. But I wasn't sure you would have me without him..."

"It's all good, Freedom," Ivy replied. "I want you here, you. You're home now."

Ivy leaned in and the two kissed. The relief Freedom felt was overwhelming. He wrapped his arms around Ivy and pulled her closer, kissing her intensely.

When Ivy pulled away, she smiled.

"There's someone I want you to meet!"

"Oh really," Freedom replied seeing a spark in Ivy's eyes.

On cue, Assent walked into the room.

"Hello, Freedom, I'm Assent," Assent said smiling. "Ivy's told me so much about you."

Assent crossed the room and Freedom appreciated her entirely. She sat down on the bed next to him and leaned over offering a kiss. Freedom readily accepted it.

"Hi..."

Ivy crawled in the bed next to Freedom and Assent settled in next to her placing her head in Ivy's lap. Ivy was flanked on both sides by two people who thought the world of her. She cared a lot about them too. Ivy smiled as she stroked Assent's thick mane. Freedom leaned against Ivy's shoulder and nestled further down in the bed. No words were exchanged just gentle caresses between the newly forming trio. She thought about her dad and the smile on her face broadened.

Hope you're happy, old man, Ivy thought to herself as she appreciated her surroundings. Ivy did what her father told her she should do. Ivy settled down, in her own way of course. She was, after all, her father's daughter...

The End